Bedtime Stories for Adults Collection

Relaxing Sleep Stories, Hypnosis & Guided Meditations for Deep Sleep, Mindfulness, Overcoming Anxiety, Panic Attacks, Insomnia & Stress Relief

© Copyright 2020 - All rights reserved.

The content contained within this book may not be reproduced, duplicated or transmitted without direct written permission from the author or the publisher.

Under no circumstances will any blame or legal responsibility be held against the publisher, or author, for any damages, reparation, or monetary loss due to the information contained within this book; either directly or indirectly.

Legal Notice:

This book is copyright protected. This book is only for personal use. You cannot amend, distribute, sell, use, quote or paraphrase any part, or the content within this book, without the consent of the author or publisher.

Disclaimer Notice:

Please note the information contained within this document is for educational and entertainment purposes only. All effort has been executed to present accurate, up to date, and reliable, complete information. No warranties of any kind are declared or implied. Readers acknowledge that the author is not engaging in the rendering of legal, financial, medical or professional advice.

Table of Contents

INTRODUCTION 1

DEEP SLEEP GUIDED MEDITATIONS AND HYPNOSIS 2

    20-MINUTE DEEP SLEEP BREATHING TECHNIQUE 2

    THE GUIDING LIGHT – 30 MINUTE STRESS-RELIEVING MEDITATION 8

    YOUR OWN PIECE OF HEAVEN – GUIDED VISUALIZATION FOR A RELAXING SLEEP 16

    30-MINUTE THINKING-TO-FANTASY SLEEP HYPNOSIS . 24

    NIGHT WALKING – GUIDED RELAXATION FOR SLEEP ... 32

    COUNTING BLESSINGS FOR INSOMNIA 39

    PRE-SLEEP MINDFULNESS MEDITATION 47

    THE MAGICAL RIDE – ANXIETY RELIEVING SLEEP MEDITATION 52

BEDTIME STORIES 60

    THE NEW ZEELAND'S HOUSE 60

    DAYDREAMING IN THE OFFICE 67

    THE SECRET RECIPE 71

    FAREWELL, CITY LIGHTS! 85

    THE 18TH CENTURY BEAUTY 99

CHASING A DREAM	106
THE SILVER NOTEBOOK	117
ALL ABOARD THE NIGHT TRAIN	130
CHAIN OF ROCKS	137
CONCLUSION	**144**

Introduction

If sleep seems impossible to reach and the minutes grow longer and longer, you are in desperate need of something to speed up the process. And while popping pills may seem like the shortcut that will get you unconscious without a failure, the side-effects that these medications drag with them are definitely not worth it. Cannot find a healthy way to catch some Zs on your own? That's why this book is here for!

Let us tell you a story! Not one that will leave you biting your nails all night, impatient to find out how it ends. But one that tells a narrative in the most hypnotizing way possible. A story, perfectly designed for your bedtime routine. Just like the fairytales that lulled your younger-self to sleep, these adult bedtime stories will do the same for you now.

And if that's not enough for you to put your headphones off and get ready to doze off, we're bringing you sleep meditations that will relieve you from stress, knockdown anxiety, stop your racing mind, and make you more mindful.

Sounds like something your tired-self could benefit from? Settle into a comfortable sleeping position and let this book guide you to dreamland. Relaxing nights are guaranteed!

Deep Sleep Guided Meditations and Hypnosis

20-Minute Deep Sleep Breathing Technique

Duration: 20 minutes

Welcome to this 20-minute breathing meditation that will get rid of the stress that the long day has loaded you with. By calming your senses and focusing on the breath that goes in and out of your body, you will be able to stop your racing mind, unwind, and enter a deep state of relaxation. If you manage to reach the end of this meditation (unless you doze off before these 15 minutes are up), I guarantee a good night's sleep.

Let's start by settling into a comfortable position that you can easily fall asleep from. Assuming you are wearing loose-fit clothes and that you have turned off all electronics and other distractions, we can begin.

Close your eyes. Take a deep breath – as deep as you can. Hold it there for two seconds. Release very slowly through your nose. Let's do this one more time. A very deep breath in. Hold, one, two, three. Release slowly through the nose.

And again. Pay attention to your breath, how it fills your lungs, how your chest feels. When taking such a deep breath, this area feels tense, as it is about to burst open. When breathing out, notice the relaxing sensation that happens here. The release of breath brings comfort back to this area. Your chest deflates, your lungs shrink back to normal. The tension is gone.

That is why deep breathing is soothing because of that calm feeling that you get to experience over and over. Let's try it one more time. A deep breath in. Feel the energy there, the tension. Breathe out slowly, focusing on the gradual comfort that fills this area.

Another deep breath in. Hold for one, two, three. Let it out slowly through your nose.

Now, keep breathing like that, without focusing on anything in particular. Just acknowledge the presence of your breath. Feel it in your nostrils, in your lungs, but just to know it's there. The important thing is to keep going with this deep breathing technique but allow your mind to find its way to relaxation.

I will now count to 20 very slowly, and you will keep on breathing. Deeply, calmly, gently. Just keep your focus float around, and allow your mind to unwind on its own.

1, 2, 3, 4, 5, 6, 7, 8, 9, 10, 11, 12, 13, 14, 15, 16, 17, 18, 19, 20.

Breathe in deeply. Hold, one two. Breathe out slowly.

Breathe in. Hold for one, two. Breathe out.

Breathe in. Breathe out.

Breathe in. Breathe out.

If a particular thought pops up, let it. Acknowledge its presence, know it is there. Do not judge yourself. Don't allow it to get between you and the equilibrium that is waiting for you to arrive. Your busy mind and unwanted thoughts shouldn't keep you from resting and being calm. But they shouldn't be ignored either, as that is counterproductive.

For you to truly be able to unwind, you have to choose not to obsess over your thoughts. Ignoring them will only backfire. So, when a feeling or idea blocks your path to relaxation, acknowledge it, but without getting into details.

Very gently, take a deep breath again. Only this time, when breathing out slowly through your nose, imagine your thought leaving your mind like the breath is leaving your body. Know that the idea, feeling is there, and then simply breathe it out. If it helps, visualize this process by giving these thoughts and feelings color.

If the thought is positive, give it a bright color. If it is negative, make it black. Whether positive or not, at this moment, you wish to be free. So, whatever pops into your head, breathe it out.

Take a deep breath and hold it for one, two, acknowledging the thought. Now, exhale slowly through the nose, imagining the color getting out of your nostrils, leaving your mind and disappearing into thin air.

Once you get rid of your disruptive thoughts, very gently return your focus to your breath to kind of "erase" these images for good.

Just breathe in. And out. In and out.

Let's try deep breathing again. A deep breath in. Hold it for two seconds. Release slowly through your nose.

A deep breath in. 1, 2, 3 A slow breath out.

A deep breath in. 1, 2, 3 A slow breath out.

Deeply in. Wait for one, two. Slowly out.

Keep on breathing without thinking about anything in particular. Allow your breath to transport you to another dimension, detaching you from the reality of your past day, completely. Try not to engage in any thoughts or images that may pop up. Simply shrug everything off by re-shifting your sole attention to the way in which the breath enters and leaves your nostrils. Try to feel the air there. Focus on the sensation that happens inside. Stay with your breath.

As I count to 30, you will keep on breathing, allowing the breath to relax your whole being.

1, 2, 3, 4,5 ,6, 7, 8, 9, 10, 11, 12, 13, 14, 15, 16, 17, 18, 19, 20, 21, 22, 23, 24, 25, 26, 27, 28, 29, 30.

You are feeling more and more relaxed.

With each breath, you are getting calmer and calmer.

One, two, three…

The profound equilibrium is right in front of you. It is almost like you can step inside.

Slowly, gently… sinking deeply… feeling heavier… and heavier..

Breathing slowly… gently…

Sleepy… tired…

Drifting off…

The Guiding Light – 30 Minute Stress-Relieving Meditation

Duration: 30 minutes

Welcome to this 30-minute sleep meditation that will help you get rid of stress and anxiety, and allow you to approach deep-sleep relaxation in the most carefree way possible. Without the thoughts and feelings that bring duress, your mind will be free to wander, allowing your whole being to enter complete calmness.

This is a sleep meditation. For this to work, you will have to make sure that you will not be disturbed or interrupted. You will need to lie down in your bed, making sure that the position is comfortable enough for you to eventually drift off from. Now, close your eyes. Keep your hands at your sides or on top of your belly, and let's begin.

We always start a meditation with a deep breath, as our breath is the most powerful tool that we use to knock down all of the intense emotions and feelings, and allow ourselves to think about something else for a second – how good it feels to be relaxing.

So, through your nose, inhale as deeply as possible. Now very gently, allow your breath to come out.

A deep breath in. A slow one out.

Inhaling deeply. Exhaling slowly.

Feel the sensation that happens in your nostrils when breathing in and out. Allow yourself to feel the presence of the breath.

A deep breath in. A slow breath out.

Breathing in. And out. In and out. Inhale and exhale.

Now, very slowly, return to normal breathing. Do not think about anything in particular. Just lie down with your breath, not focusing on anything specific. I will now count to 20, and you will allow yourself to feel or think about whatever takes over.

1, 2, 3, 4, 5, 6, 7, 8, 9, 10, 11, 12, 13, 14, 15, 16, 17, 18, 19, 20.

Have your mind wandered off somewhere you wouldn't want it to be? When our days are stressed and our minds preoccupied, every moment of silence is a chance to creep back into the darkness. That is why we cannot fall asleep easily. But instead of fighting it, or tossing and turning, we will now accept the stressful and negative emotions and choose to move past them.

So, whatever sensation has taken over, allow yourself to feel it. It is a part of your days, so you shouldn't ignore it. Know it is there, reminding you that there are tons of unfinished chores, things you should be thinking about. Spend a few moments acknowledging how this makes you feel.

Now, think of all those feelings, thoughts, and emotions as black spots. But instead of them being present in your mind only, imagine these sensations wrapping themselves all around you. Spot by spot, slowly, this blackness has surrounded you completely.

Try to imagine yourself standing outside, and the blackness just growing all around you. It is not night, but for you, it is pitch black. You cannot see a thing. That is caused by your stress and anxiety. That is what destructive feelings do. Once you allow them to pile up inside, you are stuck in the dark.

But you don't want to be feeling that way. You need joy, light. You need to be feeling relaxed, content, happy. Just like you've allowed yourself to feel the stress, now, try to push it down. Think of something better for a change. Think of things that make you feel good. Things that bring a smile to your face.

Like enjoying a popsicle on a hot summer day. Dipping your toes into the sand on your favorite beach. Going for a trip around the world. Seeing Paris.

Whatever it is that makes you feel good, try to focus your whole begin on that sensation in this moment. The blackness is still there, but once you bring the good feelings to the mix, you see a glimpse of light.

Focus on these positive emotions. As you are thinking more and more about the things that put you in a relaxing mood, the stress will lose its intensity and will slowly start to fall behind.

I will now count to 20 again, but this time, put your attention on the good things. The feelings that bring joy. Imagine scenarios, relieve positive memories, it doesn't matter. The point is for you to *feel* how good it is when your mind is not focused on stressful and anxious emotions.

1, 2, 3, 4, 5, 6, 7, 8, 9, 10, 11, 12, 13, 14, 15, 16, 17, 18, 19, 20.

Now that you see how rewarding ditching the stress aside can be, imagine yourself walking towards the light. Start walking very slowly, gently, step by step, following this mysterious light that leads you someplace you have never been to. Although you don't know where it will take you, you trust that it is the right decision. You know this because you feel it. You feel it deep in your heart, you feel your mind becoming clearer.

So, keep walking ahead, but stay focused on the good feelings. The sensation that happens in your body when you're satisfied. How it feels to be genuinely content. No worries present, nothing to stress over. Just you and the peacefulness that surrounds you.

As you are becoming more and more aware of the power of relaxation, you see that the blackness is starting to disappear and that the light is only growing bigger and brighter.

With each step you take, it seems that the pathway becomes more and more illuminated. You feel different. It is though every time you inhale you breathe calmness in. Let it fill your whole being with relaxing vibes.

Keep going ahead, following the growing light, thinking about nothing but good things. Feel the burden growing smaller – there are not that many of the black spots left behind. Your steps are now lighter, more confident. Nothing is weighing you down. You feel light and free as a bird.

As you keep going towards the light, try to complement your good thoughts with relaxing breathing. Remember that the breath is the most relieving tool, so use it as a weapon to shatter the darkness.

Breathe slowly and gently, while imagining yourself walking ahead, the light in front of you getting brighter.

A deep breath through your nose, a slow breath out.

Inhale deeply and exhale slowly.

As I count to 10, focus on your breath and the feelings that overpower the stress at this point.

1, 2, 3, 4, 5, 6, 7, 8, 9, 10.

Keep going ahead. You are almost there. The light has grown so big, that you can barely even see the few black spots left. Just a few more steps. A few more steps and you will have arrived at your mysterious destination. Don't give up now.

One step ahead, two steps forward, three steps ahead, four steps ahead, five steps forward, six steps forward, seven steps ahead…almost there.

Breathe in and out slowly and gently.

Inhale and exhale.

In and out.

Feel the breath in your chest and nostrils, feel your lungs expand and deflate.

Feel how good it is to be free of thoughts, free of worries, free of destructive emotions.

Glowing brighter and brighter with each step, you can no longer see the ball of light ahead. Now, there is lightness everywhere. No stressful feelings left, no black spots visible.

You have entered a new dimension. You feel different now. Tired of your trip, your legs are becoming heavier, you feel as though your whole body will be swallowed by the ground you are standing on.

Everything is peaceful around you, beautiful, almost dreamy. And yet, you struggle to keep your eyes open. Your eyeballs are so heavy, that all there's left for you to do is close them. You find a cool shade under a tree and decide to sit down, just to relax.

Imagine yourself leaning back with your eyes closed, thinking about nothing in particular, just allowing the heaviness to subside on its own. Your breath is gentle, slow, harmonized. Your mind is clear, your body craves rest.

Now shift back to how you're really feeling. Feel your heavy body lying in bed. Focus on the weight that is pressing into the mattress, your bed getting ready to swallow it. Let it. Allow yourself to fall deeper and deeper.

It almost feels as you're traveling down a pit. But it feels so good to be able to give your being the chance to rest. Your arms, your legs, your eyes, your head, even your mind, they all feel the need to be without movement, without activity – to simply unwind and be at peace.

You're feeling sleepier, heavier. Your mind is ready to doze off. Ready to allow yourself the chance to recharge and rest.

Nothing is bothering you now. You think about nothing. Feel the heaviness pressing into the bed, and allow the weight to transport you to another dimension.

Someplace where you relax. Someplace when there is nothing but tranquility.

Drifting off…

Almost there…

Sleep.

Your Own Piece of Heaven – Guided Visualization for a Relaxing Sleep

Duration: 30 minutes

We all need a safe haven. Someplace where we can escape to whenever we need to relax and unwind. Someplace we feel secure and shielded from the troubles of the world. A place where we truly belong. This 30-minute meditation helps you create your own imaginary heaven – somewhere you can visit before going to sleep to knock down the anxiety and helo your whole being relax so you can peacefully drift off and get a good night's sleep.

Before we begin, make sure that you are comfortable. I cannot stress the importance of comfort during meditation enough. If you want this script to have any success, you have to be sure that you will neither be disrupted nor will you be readjusting your position. You need to be lying still. So, take a comfortable sleeping position and close your eyes.

We will start by focusing on your breath. The breathing technique is perfect for tuning down the senses and allowing your body to relax, which is the perfect start for any meditation.

So, take a deep breath through your nose. Hold it for a couple of seconds, then release it through the nose again, but very slowly.

Do it again. A deep breath in Hold for one, two, then breathe out slowly.

And again. Inhale as deeply as you can, hold the breath for two seconds, then breathe it out through the nose.

A deep breath in. Hold for one, two. Breathe out slowly.

I will count to 20, and you will continue with this breathing technique to snap out of your surroundings and enter a more relaxing state.

1, 2, 3, 4, 5, 6, 7, 8, 9, 10, 11, 12, 13, 14, 15, 16, 17, 18, 19, 20.

Now that you are calmer and more in control of your emotions, let's find your dreamy place.

Imagine yourself walking down a long and sandy beach. It is a lovely spring day. The weather is just perfect - sunny, but not hot for a walk. You love the fact that you are alone and can truly enjoy yourself. You needed this for a long time. You needed to be away from your daily worries and stresses. You had to put all thoughts aside, just for a moment, and spend this time on your own. Not thinking about things that frustrate you, not letting anxiety take over your emotions.

And so you walk on, step by step, your bare feet gently pressing into the warm sand. Sinking into the softness. The grainy texture on the skin gives you comfort. It feels good to be walking on the beach.

The sun warms your face, your arms, your legs. There is a slight breeze, enough to bring some waves your way. Imagine yourself listening to the sound of the ocean. Imagine getting closer to the water, allowing the foam to gently touch your feet. Feel the breeze on your skin as well. Light and refreshing. Making you feel peaceful. Allowing you to be your true self. There is no pretending, there is no need to prove anything at this moment. You are not working on anything, you are not trying to please anyone—only yourself. Treat yourself with this walk.

And so you keep going, breathing gently, slowly, relaxed. In and out. In and out.

Breathe in. Breathe out.

Breathe in. Breathe out.

Step by step. In and out. Slowly. Gently.

Think about how this moment feels. Transport yourself to this scenario, Try to feel yourself being there. Imagine the sounds, think about the scent of the sea. Feel the refreshing breeze and the warm sun dance around your skin.

Breathe in. Breathe out.

Just when you thought that this couldn't get any more satisfying, you spot something in the distance. You are not quite sure what it is, but you increase the pace to get there quickly. You are curious. Eager to find out.

You are getting closer and closer, the object growing bigger and bigger until you finally realize that it is a door. At, what seems to be the end of the beach, there is a door. You can see that there is greenery behind that door, but there is no way to reach it except to go through it.

You start hesitating, unsure of what to do, but you end up putting your hand on the knob anyway. You want to find out what's on the other side of it. You try opening it, but without any luck. The door is locked.

You look around as if you are sure that you will find something to open it with. But there is nothing but sand. Just when you are getting ready to turn around and go back, you see something shiny next to your right foot. It is the key.

You take the warm key in your hand and put it into the lock. Once you release it, you push the door open.

You are stunned. The view is picture-perfect. Dreamy. Almost too magnificent to be true. The first thing that catches your eyes is the lush green grass, trees... The greenness is everywhere. There are hundreds of different shades of colors to break and complement the green background, and you realize that those are all flowers. There are birds – blue, yellow, red – singing the most beautiful melody – the best treat for your ears. There are colorful butterflies everywhere. This place is pure heaven – and only you have the key to open it.

You decide to enter. You are still barefoot, so the moment you transition from the war and to the cool grass, you notice the refreshing sensation, not only in your feet, toes, but feel it rising all the way up to your spine. You shut the door behind you and decide to spend a few relaxing moments in this surreal equilibrium.

So you start walking ahead, exploring the wonders that your own piece of heaven has to offer. Feel the moist grass under your feet, imagine the colorful birds, butterflies, flowers focus on the lovely chirping. Try to really put yourself there. Imagining how that might feel. What sensations may take over at that moment. Feel your presence in such a heavenly place. And do it all while breathing slowly and calmly, allowing yourself to get more and more transported there with each breath.

Breathing slowly. Gently. In and out. In and out.

I will now count to 30, allowing you the time to find your heaven and feel yourself relaxing and unwinding there.

1, 2, 3, 4, 5, 6, 7, 8, 9, 10.

You are still there. Walking on the fresh and moist grass.

11, 12, 13, 14, 15, 16, 17, 18, 19, 20.

Still walking and walking. Enjoying yourself being there.

21, 22, 23, 24, 25, 26, 27, 28, 29, 30.

You continue ahead, noticing how the lush meadow is getting narrower at the top. And at that narrow point, this place looks even more heavenly. So you start walking ahead, step by step, eager to get there.

One by one, your feet keep pressing against the cool surface. The blades gently tickling, the humid grass refreshing on the skin. Your breath is balanced, calm, and slow. You inhale through your nose and exhale very slowly.

In through your nose. Out through the nose again.

Breathe in. Breathe out. In and out.

The whole ambiance is soothing and reassuring. It is calming your senses, allowing them to let go of everything and put their entire focus on the stunning surroundings. The grass, the trees, the flowers… The vibrant colors that are all around you. The air of freshness, the scent of nature. Imagine how you would really feel in that situation. Walking down this meadow, taking in its pacifying beauty

Breathe gently and allow your breath to unravel these easing emotions withing you. Let them come to life. Here and now.

Breathe in. Breathe out.

Breathe in, and breathe out.

In and out. Gently, slowly.

You have finally reached the narrow tip. There is an old tree there. Imagine yourself sitting down and leaning back. As you do so, all of a sudden, you realize that there has been this heaviness in your legs.

Craving rest. Pleased to be finally in a relaxing position.

Allow that heavy feeling to consume you. Feel it everywhere. In your legs, arms, down your spine, on your eyelids... Everything feels tired. Imagine yourself closing your eyes and finding a comfortable position.

The chirping is still there. So is the warm sun, gentle breeze, the lovely scent. Allow yourself to be lulled to sleep by the mesmerizing nature. Softening your senses, relaxing your whole being.

Drifting off to sleep... slowly... surely...

You are so heavy, it almost feels as though you are sinking...

Deeper and deeper...

Allowing the heaviness to completely take over...

Dozing off now...

Almost there...

Ready to fall into a deep state of relaxation...

Sleep...

30-Minute Thinking-to-Fantasy Sleep Hypnosis

Duration: 30 minutes

Those who cannot fall asleep easily usually spend a lot of time in the thinking zone. Replaying scenarios of the past day, trying to find solutions for the future troubles, stressing over chores… If you cannot allow your mind to shift from thinking to fantasy on its own, then this self-hypnosis meditation will help you switch off.

Just like with any sleep meditation or hypnosis, start by lying down in your bed, finding a comfortable position that you can undisturbedly fall asleep from. Make sure to keep your hands still, either by your sides, between the thighs, or on your belly. Next, close your eyes. Remember that this is a meditation that will allow you to drift off, you wouldn't want to be interrupted by your surroundings. Assuming that you are comfortable, we can now proceed.

Remember, this is not a magic bullet – there is no way for you to count to ten and enter the hypnoidal stage. That is simply not possible. What this meditation can do for you, though, is train your mind not to force itself out of the thinking zone and counterproductively fall back into it again, but to allow it to happen, relax, welcome fantasy, and transport yourself through the hypnoidal to the deep sleep stage. And that can only be achieved by practicing. So, let's begin.

You are lying in your bed. You are feeling comfortable. Getting ready to sleep. Or at least trying to. You are human, though. Certain thoughts will appear and take over your mind. Let them. At this point, allow them to consume your energy. We are trying to train your mind to choose to step away from them, so you can not only fall asleep tonight, tomorrow, or during this practice, but develop a long-term skill that will help you dwindle the power of your thoughts and fight off insomnia.

So, keep lying peacefully with your eyes closed, not thinking or focusing on anything in particular. I will not count to 30, and you will just vaguely acknowledge the counting, not putting your attention on the numbers. Just be here at this moment, and allow yourself to feel, think.

1, 2, 3, 4, 5, 6, 7, 8, 9, 10, 11, 12, 13, 14, 15, 16,1 7, 18, 19, 20, 21, 22, 23, 24, 25, 26, 27, 28, 29, 30.

Whether your feelings are good or bad, your active participation in the thinking process keeps you away from the hypnoidal stage. But, to get there, you first need to pass through the fantasy land.

However, there are no thoughts allowed in fantasyland. You need to leave them behind. Now that you know what your feelings and emotions are about, you can choose not to engage in them and shift your focus to something else instead. In this case, that would be imaginary feel-good scenarios.

So, I will now count to 20, and you will do nothing in particular. Whatever comes to your mind, allow it.

1, 2, 3, 4, 5, 6, 7, 8, 9, 10, 11, 12, 13, 14, 15, 16, 17, 18, 19, 20.

Now that the thoughts and emotions are there, try to turn away from there.

I do not want to be thinking about this now.

I want to relax.

I deserve to go someplace nice and cozy.

I am tired. I wish to be able to unwind and rest.

I do not want to engage in these emotions now.

I am putting all of it aside, allowing my whole being to find peace.

I will count to 20 again, but this time, if something comes to your mind, tell yourself that you do not wish to engage and shrug it off.

1, 2, 3, 4, 5, 6, 7, 8, 9, 10, 11, 12, 13, 14, 15, 16, 17, 18, 19, 20.

Now, take a deep breath and think of something that soothes you. A pleasant memory from the past can be a great anchor that will restore the balance of your troubled mind. Allow yourself to go back to when things were simpler, peaceful. Try to find a memory that will bring positive feelings and instantly uplift the mood. This is not only done so that you can relax, but also because fantasizing is the prequel to being in hypnosis.

Think of something that calms you down. Perhaps watching your kids laugh, cuddling with your pet, spending a hot afternoon on the beach, skiing down a mountain, dancing with your partner. .. Whatever calms your senses, place your entire focus there.

Again, I will count to 20, and now, you will think about this thing that calms you down.

1, 2, 3, 4, 5, 6, 7, 8, 9, 10, 11, 12, 13, 14, 15, 16, 17, 18, 19, 20.

Increase the intensity of these emotions by recreating or inventing scenarios. Let's say you are on the beach. Try to feel your presence there. Imagine that you are not in bed at this moment – you are lying on the sand, with your legs placed next to the water. Imagine each wave gently touching the skin on your legs, providing a refreshing sensation, leaving foamy bubbles on the surface. Feel yourself gently tilting your head back, allowing the sunlight to leave warm trails all over your face. Focus on the sound of the crashing waves, feel the presence of the nearby seagulls. Let your fingers and toes sink into the sand, feel the grainy texture. Let this moment bring you comfort and calmness. You are safe, secure, alone, relaxed. You get to be you. No need for overthinking things, no room for stress. You have this time only for yourself. So tend to your needs. And right now, you need *this.* You need this freedom – you need the feeling of peacefulness. Enjoy it!

[pause]

Stay focused on this moment. Without overthinking it. Without putting your attention on anything in particular. Just notice the relaxing sensation and allow yourself to be lying on the beach, calm and free.

I will now count to 20 again, and you will stay in this moment, thinking about how good it feels to be this relaxed.

1, 2, 3, 4, 5, 6, 7, 8, 9, 10, 11, 12, 13, 14, 15, 16, 17, 18, 19, 20.

Breathe slowly, and imagine yourself breathing on the beach. You are still there. Nothing is changed.

Just keep breathing very gently, allowing your breath to transport you to your dreamy place. Feel the warmth, the refreshing touch of the ocean. Inhale slowly and deeply, and when you exhale, just notice how each breath relaxes you even more. [pause] And more. [pause]. And more.

You are slowly reaching for the hypnoidal stage. Almost there. Let your breaths take you there. Let each wave be the indicator that your total equilibrium is just a few steps away. Let it come close to you. Without trying too hard. Without stressing over it. Just let your mind drift off naturally. All you have to do at this moment is stay relaxed.

Take a deep breath. Feel the sun on your face, Exhale very slowly. 1, 2, 3. Now feel the ocean on your legs, so refreshing. Let's do it again.

A deep breath goes in. The sun warms you up. Let the breath out slowly through your nose. Now hear the wave kiss the sand, then touch your skin gently. Feel the cool sensation, not only in your legs but up your spine, all the way through your head. It seems as though the ocean can also cool off the warm touch that the sun leaves on your cheeks.

And again. A deep breath goes in. Notice the sun, the sound the ocean makes. Exhale in 1, 2, 3. Allow the calming sensation to pierce deeper and deeper. To tranquil your whole being.

Feel yourself getting heavier, feel the muscles relax completely. You are almost there.

Stay in this moment, relaxed, free, calm. And just breathe. In and out. In and out.

Breathe in. Breathe out.

Breathe in. Breathe out.

You are now traveling to the land of deep hypnosis. I will count to 10, and by the time we reach the number ten, you will be in a conscious sleep.

1, 2, 3, 4, 5, 6, 7, 8, 9, 10.

You have arrived. Everything feels different here. Lighter, better, carefree. You can stay like this for hours. Don't fight your urge to enjoy it. Just breathe.

Remember your time on the beach and let your breath, going in and out, bring you closer to a deep state of unconsciousness, slowly, surely, step by step.

Almost there. Keep breathing. A deep breath in. A slow breath out.

Breathe in. And then breathe out.

Breathe in. Breathe out.

Slowly, calmly, peacefully.

Breathe in. Breathe out.

I will count to 20, and you will use this time to stay on your breath, allowing it to bring deep relaxation your way.

Get ready to doze off. Completely. Unconsciously.

1, 2, 3, 4, 5, 6, 7, 8, 9, 10, 11, 12, 13, 14, 15, 16, 17, 18, 19, 20.

Sleepy…

Heavy…

Drifting off…

Sleep.

Night Walking – Guided Relaxation for Sleep

Duration: 25 minutes

When we lie in bed, we cannot possibly expect to simply tune off from our surroundings or stop our mind from replaying things and images from the busy day. We are humans – not machines. We sense things, we feel, and we do so deeply. To be able to bring comfort and relaxation to our body and mind, we need to allow ourselves the time to let the stress subside. We need to gradually enter the stage of calmness without rushing it. And this meditation will do just that – allow you to relax by the power of guided visualizations. So, let's begin.

Lie down in your bed and find a comfortable position. Make sure to turn off all electronics and get rid of distractions, to make sure that nothing will interrupt this practice. Then, close your eyes.

Let's start by focusing on the breath. Breathing is a powerful technique that relaxes. Allowing the oxygen to flow to the brain freely, and acknowledging the sensation in the meantime can do wonders.

So, take a deep breath slowly through the nose. Let it fill your lungs, feel them expand. Hold it there for two seconds, feeling the tension almost piercing through. Let go through the nose again, very slowly, paying attention on how your lungs shrink.

One more time. Take a deep breath, as deep as you can. Hold it there for one, two, then release slowly through the nose, noticing the sensation in your belly.

And again. A deep breath goes in. Hold it there for two seconds. Then exhale slowly through the nose, feeling your belly soften and deflate.

Breathe in. Hold, one, two. Breathe out.

Breathe in. Hold for two seconds. Breathe out slowly.

In and out. [pause]

In and out. [pause]

Now that you are not so tensed anymore, follow me on a powerful visualizing guided walk outside. It may seem odd at this moment, but imagining yourself walking in the dark can not only distract you from your thoughts and allow you to relax, but it will also send strong signals to your brain and help you fall asleep easily.

Imagine yourself standing outside. It is nighttime. The weather is chilly, but not too cold for a walk. The slight breeze present provides freshness and the fact that you are alone comfort. You are walking down a path that is unfamiliar to you. And with each step you take, you realize that your surroundings are slowly starting to fade away.

There are stores, buildings, streets all around you, but with each second that passes, they become less and less visible.

It is an odd sensation. It feels strange, weird even. But you are not afraid. Nor curious as to why the things that surround you seem to be disappearing. Quite the contrary. The fact that they are fading away is comforting. It makes you feel alive somehow. Free to be yourself.

So keep walking ahead, allowing everything around you to vanish. Don't focus on that; instead, keep your breathing balanced and calm, and keep going forward.

Breathe in. Breathe out.

One step ahead. Two steps ahead.

Breathe in. Breathe out.

Breathe in. Breathe out.

Step by step by step by step.

I will now slowly count to twenty, and you will continue breathing calmly, imagining yourself walking down a path where everything seems to be disappearing from sight.

1, 2, 3, 4, 5, 6, 7, 8, 9, 10, 11, 12, 13, 14, 15, 16, 17, 18, 19, 20.

There is nothing around you now. Long fields stretched all around you, with nothing else in your view. The twinkling stars above your head look like millions of diamonds hung to the deep and dark sky. The moon has never looked brighter to you, and it is the only thing that illuminates your way. But you don't need anything else. There is nothing to trip over, nothing to pay attention to. Only you, and this dark beauty.

So you keep on going. You don't know where this path leads, but it is the only way you can go. You are not obsessing over what you might find at the end of it. Instead, you are enjoying the walk. Slowly, freely, comfortably.

Keep going ahead, and try to really see yourself outside now. Walking in the dark. Alone and free. Let your breath transport you there.

Breathe in. Breathe out.

Breathe in. And breathe out.

The wind is harsher now, it seems. It is no more refreshing. Instead, you feel colder and colder. Goosebumps cover your arms, legs, neck... Imagine what feeling cold outside in the dark may feel like.

But you keep on going.

Step by step by step.

Breathing in. And breathing out. In and out.

Your legs are also getting heavier. The long walk has been tiring, and all you want to do now is to lie down, throw something over to warm yourself up, and fall into a relaxing sleep.

Your eyes are also getting tired – keeping them open is a struggle. But you cannot stop now. You have to keep on going and reach the end of the pathway. You cannot see it, but you can feel that it is near.

So you keep on moving forward. All you want to do now is just curl up and allow your whole being to slowly drift away. You're still breathing calmly and slowly, but you notice that even your breath has become heavier. Almost there. Keep on going.

I will now count to 10, and by the time I'm finished, you will find yourself at the end of the pathway.

1, 2, 3, 4, 5, 6, 7, 8, 9, 10.

You have finally arrived. At first, it looks like there is nothing there. But once you look closely, you notice something on the floor. Something white. You sit on the ground next to it to explore it. You press onto it with your hand, and you realize that it is soft.

You are tired and cold, so you decide to lie on top of the white softness. Feel your whole body pressing into it. Deeper and deeper. You are no longer on the surface. With every second that passes, it seems as though you are sinking deeper into it, falling further from the pathway.

The more you fall, the warmer you get. The goosebumps on your arms are almost gone now – you are starting to feel light and relaxing sensation taking over. Let it. Continue breathing in a gentle manner, and keep on falling deeper until you reach unconsciousness. Until you fall into a deep state of sleep that will recharge and replenish your whole being.

To get there, all you need to do is keep on falling. You are going down very slowly, it almost feels like floating. You can barely notice that you are moving downward, but you can feel the heaviness of your body pressing into the soft pillow-like surface. With each breath you take, you are a step closer to a state of total equilibrium. So keep on breathing/

Gently and calmly, take a breath in and slowly let it out through the nose.

A breath in. You keep on falling. A breath out. Deeper and deeper.

Another breath in. Another breath out. Falling even deeper.

Detaching your mind from your body completely. Allowing it to drift away gently.

You are feeling sleepy, and sleepy, and sleepy.

Falling deeper and deeper.

Heavy and hypnoidal, you are slowly reaching a state of complete calmness.

Breathe in. Breathe out.

You breathe in and out. In and out. Deeper.

Dozing off now…

Sleep.

Counting Blessings for Insomnia

Duration: 40 minutes

If you are suffering from insomnia and cannot fall asleep due to that unnerving condition, then I strongly suggest you try this 40-minute meditation practice. With this technique, you will be able to distract your mind by giving it something almost-hypnotizing to be preoccupied with, rather than allowing negative thoughts to creep in. Similar to the good old counting sheep, this practice of counting your blessings can help you fall asleep in no time.

Just like with any other sleep meditation, we will start by finding a comfortable position. So, wearing your cozy clothes or pajamas, lie down in your bed, settling into a posture that will support a night of good sleep. Close your eyes, and let's begin.

To detach yourself from the surroundings, it is beneficial to start this meditation with a quick breathing technique to allow your mind to *reset* and find its way to peacefulness. Let's begin by taking a deep breath, but as deep as you can. You need to feel the pressure in your chest, feel the lungs almost bursting out. Now, release very slowly through the nose.

One more time. Take a deep breath, as deeply as you possibly can. Hold it there for two seconds, placing your sole focus on the chest area. And release slowly through the nose.

And again. A deep breath goes in. Hold it for two seconds, noticing the tension in your lungs and chest. Then feel them deflate when breathing out.

A deep breath in. Hold for one, two, three. Then release slowly through your nose.

Another deep breath goes in. Hold it for two seconds. Breathe out very slowly.

I will not count to 20, and you will keep on breathing deeply, with your focus placed on your chest.

1, 2, 3, 4, 5, 6, 7, 8, 9, 10, 11, 12, 13, 14, 15, 16, 17, 18, 19, 20.

Now that you are calmer and more relaxed than a few minutes ago, let's begin counting your blessings. One by one, the things you are grateful for will show you that you have incredible happiness in your life. Happiness that shouldn't be overshadowed by stress, anxiety, or disrupting thoughts that keep you up your night. Everything passes. All troubles will seize to exist. Your blessings, however, are there to hold you together. Let's go through them all and get yourself in an appreciative and feel-good mood that will slay all worries and let you fall asleep.

Starting at your toes, move your attention gently upward. Through the ankles, legs, hips, abdomen, chest, neck, all the way to your head. Go through every part of your body and see how blessed you are to be here at this moment. Alive and healthy. Feel the gratitude you have for your overall health and spend a few moments thinking about this deep appreciation. As I count to 10, you will become more and more aware that your health is the single most important thing in your life – and you have it.

1, 2, 3, 4, 5, 6, 7, 8, 9, 10.

Take a deep breath. Hold for two seconds. Release slowly through the nose.

Take another deep breath. Hold it for one, two, three. Then breathe out slowly.

Now, think about the bed you are lying in. The warmth of the covers, the softness of your pillow, the support that your mattress gives. Think about how happy you are to have a bed to sleep in. I will count to 10, and you will feel the gratitude you have for the comfort of your bed.

1, 2, 3, 4, 5, 6, 7, 8, 9, 10.

Again, a deep breath goes in. Hold it there, feel the tension in your chest. Release through your nose.

A deep breath goes in. Hold it for one, two, three. Breathe out slowly through the nose.

Now, think about your room, your house. Your shelter. Think about the ability to sleep and relax freely, without having to worry about your security. Think about the gratitude you feel towards this ability. I will count to 10, and you will place your focus on this appreciation.

1, 2, 3, 4, 5, 6, 7, 8, 9, 10.

Take a deep breath now. Hold it there for two seconds. Release slowly.

Breathe in. Hold for one, two, three. Breathe out slowly.

Breathe in deeply. Hold for two seconds. Let it out slowly through the nose.

Think about your job. About your profession, the things you do for a living. Don't obsess over the job or the work activities, but merely acknowledge the fact that you do work. You are capable of providing for yourself and maybe your family. You have the ability to get things done. Think about the fact that you're lucky enough not to have to worry about that. Find the gratitude for that deep inside.

1, 2, 3, 4, 5, 6, 7, 8, 9, 10.

Brethe deeply and gently. In and out. In and out.

Feel the breath in your chest, the tension that is there. Feel it releasing when you breathe out slowly through your nose.

And again, take a deep breath. Hold it for two seconds. And then slowly let it go.

Think about the love you have in your life. About your family and friends. The healthy relationships you have. The strong bond that holds you and the people you care about connected. Think about the fact that you are not alone in this world. You have someone that thinks about you and wishes you well. I will now count to 30, and you will use that time to think about the people in your life that are most important to you. Think about how blessed you are for them.

1, 2, 3, 4, 5, 6, 7, 8, 9, 10, 11, 12, 13, 14, 15, 16, 17, 18, 19, 20, 21, 22, 23, 24, 25, 26, 27, 28, 29, 30.

Take a deep breath again. Hold for two seconds, then slowly breathe it out through the nose.

Do this one more time. [pause]

Now think about your education, the things you know, the things you have learned through your life. The experiences you've gained, the skills you have attained. Think about how grateful you are for them. How appreciative you feel that no one will be able to take that away from you. How you will use your talent and knowledge to grow and achieve more in your life. Think about that for 10 seconds.

1, 2, 3, 4, 5, 6, 7, 8, 9, 10.

You are now feeling sleepier. Your body feels heavier. You feel it pressing into the mattress. It almost feels like you're sinking into the bed. But we are not done yet. So much more to be grateful for.

Think about all of the places you have been lucky enough to visit. The things you have been able to see. So many beautiful sights have found a permanent spot in your memory, allowing you to revisit whenever you feel the need for it.

In your mind, express gratitude for the things you have seen, as I slowly count to 10.

1, 2, 3, 4, 5, 6, 7, 8, 9, 10.

Refocus by taking a deep breath. Hold it for one, two, three. Release slowly through your nose.

A deep breath goes in. One, two seconds. Out it leaves your body slowly.

Finally, think about the ability to sleep. Be grateful for the chance you have to lie in your bed without being interrupted, and just allow your mind to slowly drift away, take its time, and find its own way to a deep calmness. Without rushing things, without forcing yourself to sleep. Just be here at this moment, and allow each second, each breath, to take you further and further away from the reality. Let yourself doze off slowly and gently, but deeply.

1, 2, 3, 4, 5, 6, 7, 8, 9, 10, 11, 12, 13, 14, 15, 16, 17, 18, 19, 20.

Breathing in gently. Breathing out slowly.

Breathe in. Breathe out.

Breathe in. Breathe out.

In and out. In and out.

Think about the exhaustion that takes over. Feel the heaviness of your body, the tired eyelids. Try to feel your whole being craving rest. Focus on the ability to provide comfort to your body while lying in your bed. Appreciate the chance you have to straighten out your spine and allow your head to rest peacefully onto your soft pillow. You are truly blessed. Don't ever forget that.

So, keep breathing, and don't fight the feelings that keep piling up inside. Without forcing or rushing things, allow yourself to find a state of deep relaxation at your own pace. Just be here, feel every sensation that happens inside, and let sleep come your way.

Let's count to 30 together, very slowly. Don't forget to keep breathing gently and calmly.

1, 2, 3, 4, 5, 6, 7, 8, 9, 10, 11, 12, 13, 14, 15, 16, 17, 18, 19, 20, 21, 22, 23, 24, 25, 26, 27, 28, 29, 30.

Your eyelids feel heavy on your eyeballs. It seems as though your arms and legs have sunken into your bed. The heaviness consumes all of you. You are feeling sleepy. Ready to doze off. Almost there.

Just keep on breathing. Breathe in. Breathe out.

Breathe in. Breathe out.

Breathe in. Breathe out.

Allow your mind to drift away. Let your body slowly follow.

Breathe in. Breathe out. Sleep.

Pre-Sleep Mindfulness Meditation

Duration: 15 minutes

The main issue with being unable to fall asleep mainly comes from the fact that you cannot detach yourself from thinking about your past or upcoming day. We often worry about obligations or replay scenarios in our head, which further engage our mind into the thinking process and keeps us away from a good night's sleep. Refocusing your attention on the present and forcing yourself to pay attention only to the things that happen in that particular moment can be the best sleep aid. Not to mention that being mindful can lead to serious other long-term benefits, as well.

Start by lying in your bed comfortably. It is important that you turn off and eliminate all distractions, so you're not disturbed during the practice. You are about to prepare yourself mentally and physically for the act of sleep, so feeling cozy is the key here. Do not close your eyes completely, but keep them half-opened.

Let's begin by taking a few deep breaths to reset your state of mind. Inhale as deeply as you can, and keep the breath there for a few seconds. Then, very slowly, breathe out through your nose.

Again – take a very deep breath, hold it for two or three seconds, then slowly let it out through the nose.

Repeat this one more time. Inhale as deeply as you possibly can, hold the breath there, keeping your chest puffed up, and then slowly feel them deflate as the breath leaves through your nostrils.

Now that you have relaxed yourself a little bit, let's continue with a more mindful technique that includes all senses. This practice will keep your mind from wandering and will prepare you for a state of calmness and deep sleep.

Let's start with your eyes. You are lying in bed with your eyes half-opened. Use them to scan your surroundings. Whatever your lying posture, try to focus on the things that you can see with your eyes at this very moment. Perhaps you're staring at the ceiling. Focus on that. Focus on the whiteness, on possible cracks you can find. Just keep your attention there for a few moments. Perhaps you are lying on your side next to your partner. Or maybe you can see out of your window. It doesn't matter. Just stay focused on what can be seen for about 20 seconds, as I slowly count to 10.

1, 2, 3, 4, 5, 6, 7, 8, 9, 10.

Now, take a deep breath, hold it there, and release slowly through your nose. You can close your eyes at this point.

Let's move on to your ears. Gently place your attention from your breath to your hearing. Focus on the things you can hear. Whatever it is, keep your attention there. Even if there is nothing but silence, focus on that. Think about how it feels not to hear anything. Keep your attention there, as I slowly count to 10.

1, 2, 3, 4, 5, 6, 7, 8, 9, 10.

Reshift to your breath now, inhaling as deeply as you can. Hold your breath there for one, two, three, and now gently let it out through the nose.

Placing your focus on your nose now, put your undivided attention on the scent. Perhaps you have an air freshener that provides a relaxing aroma. Maybe you can scent the fabric softener on your pillow. Perhaps the lotion on your skin. Whatever it is, stay focused on it.

1, 2, 3, 4, 5, 6, 7, 8, 9, 10.

Now very gently return to your breath. Breathe in very deeply, holding the breath for two seconds. Breathe out slowly through your nose.

From the breath, reshift the attention to your tongue, focusing on the taste detected in your mouth. Perhaps you have just brushed your teeth. Keep your attention on the minty taste. Think about how refreshing and clean it feels.

1, 2, 3, 4, 5, 6, 7, 8, 9, 10.

Again, take a deep breath. Hold it for one, two, three, and finally, let it out through the nose.

Turn the focus to your skin now, making sure to notice how the sense of touch feels. Your legs are touching the bed, your arms are maybe placed on your belly or thigs. Your head is on the pillow. The clothes you are wearing cover your skin. Make sure to think about these spots of individually and really try to feel the contact your skin makes with the other surfaces.

1, 2, 3, 4, 5, 6, 7, 8, 9, 10, 11, 12, 13, 14, 15, 16, 17, 18, 19, 20.

Finally, return to the breath. Only this time, do not breath deeply, but gently.

Breathe in. Breathe out.

Breathe in. Breathe out.

Inhale and Exhale. In and out.

Breathe in. Breathe out.

Now that you are more mindful about your surroundings and your mind is not where you don't want it to be, you can keep on breathing gently and stay focused on your breath until you drift off, or you can continue to a bedtime story to help you fall asleep quickly.

The Magical Ride – Anxiety Relieving Sleep Meditation

Duration: 35 minutes

A good night's sleep is hard to achieve if you're feeling anxious. When anxiety clouds your mind and takes a hold on your emotions, it can seem almost impossible to snap out of the discomfort and find your way back to relaxation. At least, you cannot do it on your own, without practice. Thankfully, that's why this technique is here for. To give you a helping hand and guide your mind and body into a state of total calmness, which you can easily fall asleep from.

This is a sleep meditation; for this practice to work, you have to be lying in your bed comfortably, as you normally do when trying to drift away. So, settle into a cozy position and make sure that there is nothing around you that can distract you. This is important as the technique will not be successful if you pause midway to answer a text or even readjust your position. That is why comfort is the key here.

Once you are sure that you will not be disturbed, close your eyes. We will start by taking a deep breath. Try to inhale as deeply as you can possibly can, allowing the breath to put some tension in your chest area. Breathe out slowly through your nose.

Again – breathe in as deeply as you can, feeling the tightness in your lungs, and then breathe out slowly, noticing how this tension softens up, and your chest deflates when exhaling.

And one more time – a deep breath goes in. Hold it there for a second, two, three. Then slowly, let it out through your nostrils.

Normally, when trying to fall asleep, you will force your mind not to think about the things that make you anxious, the thoughts that put stress on you. But now, we will do just that. Because you cannot trick your mind to simply reset – there isn't a magical button. What you can do is gradually expose it to negativity, let it get familiar with it, so you can, then, gently retrieve from it, and move back to safety. Once you are in a more comfortable zone, you can fall asleep. So, let's do just that.

Start by allowing your mind to be focused on whatever thoughts may appear to you. Don't fight the uncomfortable or anxious emotion. On the contrary – try to really sense them and notice how they make you feel.

Keep breathing very slowly, calmly, and gently. Breathing in. Breathing out. In and out. In and out.

A gentle inhale – a slow exhale. In and out. Very calmly. Just be here at this moment. Alive. With a sharp mind. Clear emotions. What are you thinking about? What are your uncertainties, fears? What makes you tossing and turning at night? What is hiding in the deepest and darkest corners of your mind? Try to get everything out in the open. Try to feel every anxious feeling that is trapped inside you.

I will now slowly count to 30, and you will stay focused on these thoughts and feelings, trying to connect with them as much as possible. Don't forget to keep breathing calmly in the meantime. If a particular image or sensation speeds up your pulse, just remember to take it easy and breathe it out.

1, 2, 3, 4, 5, 6, 7, 8, 9, 10, 11, 12, 13, 14, 15, 16, 17, 18, 19, 20, 21, 22, 23, 24, 25, 26, 27, 28, 29, 30.

Now that you know what you are feeling anxious about, try to physically get them out of your mind. Of course, that is only possible in your mind, so try to imagine yourself reaching for your thoughts and feelings, and just placing them out in the open, right beside you. You will still be able to feel and see them – they will just be outside of your body.

So, imagine your hand reaching inside, grabbing the thing you are most anxious and stressed about, and getting it out. Now, do it again. Whatever thought bothers you, whatever sensation brings feelings of doubt, uncertainty – get it all out. Even the tiniest discomforts – get them out as well. The point is for you to be able not only to take them away from your mind – the place where they can hurt you the most but also to see them for what they really are. Thoughts and feelings. Not facts, not something that you are faced with at this very moment. They are simply worries you have about something that has happened, or things that you fear will occur sometime in the future. As real as they may seem now, they have no power over you. Now, we are simply regaining that control again.

Keep reaching for things and imagine yourself placing them out in the open. It can help if you believe to be outside or somewhere where there are no space limitations, no walls, no obstacles. There, you can place as many discomforting thoughts as you'd like. There is plenty of room for your worries outside, where you are standing.

Don't forget to breathe in and out. In and out. Slowly, gently, calmly. A breath goes in. A breath goes out. Inhaling. Exhaling. In and out.

Now that everything is out in the open. Spend some time observing your anxieties, thoughts, ideas that make you feel anything less than comfortable. Do not engage in them – don't give them the power to control you mind at this point. Remember, they are not inside – you have gotten them out of your mind. You can feel their presence. You can acknowledge them well. Just, don't obsess over the details.

I will now count to 20, and you will keep standing there, breathing calmly, observing what it is that makes you feel anxious.

1, 2, 3, 4, 5, 6, 7, 8, 9, 10, 11, 12, 13, 14, 15, 16, 17, 18, 19, 20.

Now, imagine yourself walking. Take one step, then another, then another. Keep walking ahead, moving forward as if you were to escape from these feelings. You keep going and going, but it isn't enough – your thoughts and feelings follow. It isn't enough to simply turn your back to your negative emotions – you need to get far away, as quickly as possible, and get to a place where they are not invited – someplace they will not follow you to.

There is nothing else to do now, so you keep going anyway. Moving forward and forward, hoping to find a place where you can hide – someplace where you can be free of these emotions. But there is nothing outside. Just you, and the dark fog of negativity that follows you. But you keep on going. Step by step by step by step. You keep going further until you spot something – something red is waiting for you in the distance.

You pick up the pace, eager to get to that object, curious to find out what it is. So you keep on going – step by step by step, until you're finally there. You finally arrive only to find that it is nothing by a carpet lying on the floor. You wonder why someone would leave a carpet outside like that, but you decide it doesn't really matter – it cannot help you. So you decide to keep on going ahead. You make one step, another, putting your feet onto the red carpet, when all of a sudden, you notice that it is moving.

The magic carpet has lifted you from the ground; it is now flying in the air with you standing on it. You take a seat to really enjoy the ride, and you cannot help but notice how different you are feeling in this moment. You are no longer anxious, no more afraid. You turn around to see the black fog behind, but it is far in the distance. Once you have started to feel better about yourself, the anxieties subsided. They have no power – it is you who are in control, and you are just starting to see that.

So you keep on flying up in the sky. And with each second that passes, with each breath that you are slowly letting out, the anxieties seem to be further and further away.

Imagine this moment, Stay there, enjoy. Feel the wind gently touching your face while you are flying in the sky. Imagine the sensation that runs through you when you move at a comfortable speed so high in the air. You are moving away from your thoughts and anxieties until they become nothing but a black spot, a freckle almost, far in the distance.

Don't think about them now, as they have left your body and mind. All there is to do now is simply enjoy the comfort that this magical ride provides. Soothing, relaxing, liberating. I will now count to 20, and you will keep on breathing very gently, enjoying feeling this comfortable.

1, 2, 3, 4, 5, 6, 7, 8, 9, 10, 11, 12, 13, 14, 15, 16, 17, 18, 19, 20.

The ride is soothing, but you are getting tired, you feel the heaviness on your body pressing onto the carpet, applying such pressure that you have no place else to go but down, slowly and gently, you keep on lowering yourself to the ground. It almost feels as though you are floating. You are moving at such a comfortable speed that you are beginning to feel very sleepy. Your eyelids heavy, your breath even slower. You keep on going down and down, until you lower yourself to your bed. You are no longer on the carpet – you are now lying in a comfortable position in your bed.

Feeling sleepy. Craving rest.

Breathing in. And breathing out.

Slowly. Gently. One, two, three.

The heaviness keeps pressing, you are ready to let go and enter another dimension.

So tired.

Ready to drift away.

Any moment now.

Slowly. Surely.

Sleep…

Bedtime Stories

The New Zeeland's House

Duration: 30 minutes

He never thought that he would be able to visit this place again. The place where he was born. Where he took his first steps, learned how to ride a bike, fell in love with a girl for the first time. He was only thirteen when his mother got transferred from New Zeeland to Paris. He was still a kid when he was forced to learn French, leave his friends behind, go to a new school, start a whole new life someplace else. And yet, standing in front of his old house now, 30 years later, nothing looked different. Somehow, 13 didn't seem that long ago.

He still felt the same things he used to feel when he was a kid. The memories flooding his mind, the deep sensations reclaiming territory. It took a lot of strength to resist the urge to climb the old tree in the backyard. But that's not what he was here for.

In all fairness, Jake wasn't even sure why he was really here for. Perhaps it was to show his Parisian wife and almost-teenage daughter where he was coming from. To make them understand that there was more to life than Champs-Elysees and the city of light. Perhaps it was to convince himself. He had become so used to the busy lifestyle that one had to lead in Paris, that he almost erased his roots completely. He forgot all about the freedom and endless possibilities that his New Zeeland had to offer. Away from the shackles of the city, here, you could be whoever you wanted to be. Live however you felt like. And the best part of all? No one would even care. He may be accustomed to the Parisian life, but he was clearly getting tired of the judgy looks and the need to be more, earn more, achieve more. If he was being painfully honest – simplicity is what he was really looking for. That is why they agreed to maybe buying the property.

They probably spent 10 minutes staring at his old house. Him telling them stories about stray cats, bike accidents, and days spend outside with his next-door friend, and them listening carefully, glad to be seeing this new side of him. If the woman hadn't looked out the window, he would have probably spent an hour describing his childhood. For he surely had many stories to tell.

The woman, whose name was Sarah, greeted them politely. He could tell right away that she wasn't thrilled about their visit, but was kind enough to let them look around and spend some time in his old home.

"As I mentioned over the phone, I would really love to discuss the potential purchase of the house. You said that you have discussed this earlier but haven't really thought about actually putting it on the market," Jake said to Sarah.

"No, we haven't," she replied. "To be honest, I don't know how I am feeling about it. I have spent over 20 years in this house, you know. My kid grew up in this backyard, there are so many fond memories that keep me here. I am just not sure whether I will be able to find that sort of connection somewhere else. Although we really have discussed selling it. It is just too big for the two of us, and with my husband being away for work most days, it feels kind of lonely. I'd rather just own an apartment in the city." Sarah explained.

He knew exactly what she meant. About the house holding such power over you, about your need to stay there forever, holding onto these memories, like they were destined to fade away if you were to move.

"Take it from me, you will appreciate these memories, no matter where you are. We've come here because we are considering the potential move to New Zeeland. And this is where I grew up. I just think it would be fantastic if I were to move back here with my family. I don't know if you knew this, but it was my grandfather that actually build this place. So it is more sentimental for me, as you can imagine." Jake said, trying to somehow clam his right.

"I understand. If we weren't even thinking about selling it, I would have probably just refused over the phone. But I will have a good talk with my husband, and we will let you know by the end of tomorrow," Sarah promised.

He gave her a piece of paper with their offer written on it. As soon as she opened it, he noticed how her pupils increased at the generous amount. He knew very well that they priced it above the market price, but this house meant way too much for him to let the opportunity slide.

They left with a good feeling. Jake said that he wouldn't get his hopes up, but it was impossible not to. He was already feeling excited, although he very well knew that there was the possibility of Sarah and her husband refusing their offer, as generous as it may have been.

Jake and his wife, Marie, agreed they would not talk about it at all. It was best not to make any plans before they were sure that the owners of the house would be willing to sell it to them. So, instead of worrying or talking about things they were unsure of, they decided to spend the day at the beach.

Since they were in the area, Jake decided to take them to a secret spot that he frequently visited as a kid. But when they reached the destination, he was surprised to see that the place was anything but secret. A few families were enjoying the warm weather there, but the beach was so big that they had no trouble in finding a secluded place for themselves.

The ocean was crystal clear and the sandy beach so clean it was unlike anything that Marie has seen before. It was a pure, unpolluted, and untouched natural beauty. They were truly blessed to experience this. She could only imagine how amazing it would be to be able to call this place home.

Looking at how freely the teenagers were spending their days there, Jake and Marie shared a look of agreement. They didn't have to say a thing, but they both knew that moving to New Zeeland would be the right choice, even if they couldn't purchase Jake's childhood home. It was a place where their daughter Elizabeth could spend her days swimming, surfing, and enjoying the beach. Something she clearly wouldn't be able to do in Paris.

They spent a couple of hours just soaking all that beauty, and when the sun finally left their horizon, they decided it was time to call it a day and returned to the hotel they were staying at.

On their way back, Jake's phone rang. At first, he thought it was work. He was thousands and thousands of miles away from Paris, but he frequently got work-related inquiry calls. Only this time, it wasn't a peer asking for information; it wasn't a contract that needed to be sealed. Now, it was Sarah who was calling.

He gave a look that screamed *wish me luck* to Marie, and he touched the green button.

"Hi Jake, I hope I'm not disturbing you," Sarah said.

"Not at all. I am just surprised to hear from you so soon," Jake told her. He was worried that this was just a courtesy call. No one agrees on such an important decision in only two hours. This has to be a polite way to tell him that they were not planning to sell them the house.

Just as he was starting to lose all hope, Sarah said: "I am calling with good news, actually. We have agreed to accept your offer and sell the house to you."

He couldn't believe the words. All of a sudden, life got more meaningful. Everything looked brighter, better. For a split second, he wanted to tease Marie and then reveal the life-altering change that was awaiting them, but it was impossible for him to hide his ear-to-ear smile.

The next week, they made all of the arrangements, and the house was officially theirs. They gave Sarah and her husband 6 months to make the transition and move, as they were not in a hurry to move there themselves. They had quite a lot of things to take care of back in Paris.

Eight long months had passed, and Jake, Marie, and Elizabeth were standing in front of the New Zeeland's house. But unlike the last time they visited this place, they had the keys now. That and tons of boxes ready to be unpacked and placed into their new, hopefully, permanent home. Their feelings were also different. This time, they looked at this place as their home, happy for the upcoming adventures, impatient to start making new memories that will complement Jake's old ones. Because, at the end of the day, that is what's most important in life. Not where you are, but who are you with. Not the place where you will be spending your time, but the memories that you will be creating to warm up your heart for years and years to come.

Daydreaming in the Office

Duration: 15 minutes

He opened his eyes to see the most mesmerizing shade of blue just a stone-throw away. He was sitting at the most magnificent beach on earth. And it wasn't just because of the deep and crystal ocean. The whole place oozed relaxation. The sand had the finest consistency and satin-like texture he had never seen before. The palm trees were so lush and beautiful that he was actually tempted to grab a coconut, slice it in half, put a straw in, and indulge in some rich coconut water, even though he hated the flavor.

Chris was lying in a hammock, gently rocking himself and enjoying the view that spread in front of his eyes. The large palm leaves provided enough shadow to keep him from burning in the sun, but he could still feel the warmth of it on his face. It wasn't so hot that he felt the need to immediately jump into the water – the weather was actually enjoyable.

Usually, in such a situation, Chris would have a cold, sweaty drink in his hand – preferably a cocktail. Not that he was a fain of mixed drinks, but just because it perfectly fit the tropical ambiance. But, no, he didn't have a drink, nor did he need one. He was an avid reader, but he didn't have a book to read, either. He thought that giving his attention to the content of the book would feel like cheating. How could he possibly take his eyes off of this incredible sight?

He knew it was somewhere tropical, but he also somehow knew that this wasn't the Bahamas, it wasn't a Caribbean island, nor the Bermuda, Maldives, Seychelles, or any far-flung place that he could think of. He didn't know where he was, but he didn't want to, either. All that Chriss needed at this very moment was the comfort and tranquility that this place offered.

He was lying like that for, maybe, 10 minutes or so, when he decided that he actually wanted to stand up and allow his body to soak up the sunrays. So he got up, barefoot, and the first thing he noticed when his feet met the sand was the warmth of the grainy surface. Tickling his skin gently, he thought this was paradise.

He just got here from Detroit's cold and harsh winter, so you could only imagine how satisfied he was at this moment. No more shoveling snow, no more red noses, no frosty fingers. No more sweaters, boots, itchy woolen scarfs, or annoying hats. No more worrying about keeping your ears warm, no more heating, nothing. All he needed here were a few t-shirts, some shorts, and a pair of flip flops. And maybe a sun hat to protect and shield his face from the rage of the rays. Although he deeply disliked them, here, he could even wear a straw hat.

The water was tempting, calling him to jump in, but he wasn't quite sure. He liked the warmth so much that he didn't want to cool himself quite yet. But he decided to at least allow his feet to get refreshed. Walking on the wet sand near the water, he allowed the waves to gently touch his feet at regular intervals. He even sat there, lowering his body to allow the water to go up to his knees. After five minutes or so, he decided to give it a shot. He entered the water, just to realize how wrong he was all along. The water was not cold at all. If he had to choose, he would say that it was actually closer to warm. That's how good it felt to be swimming here.

And if this wasn't paradise enough, he was able to spot a couple of dolphins doing crazy backflips nearby. He felt like making a camp and never moving from this beach. For he truly believed he was in heaven.

Chris could probably spend his whole afternoon there if he wasn't interrupted by his boss. "You forgot to sign this," his boss said, handing him a piece of paper. And just like that Chris was back from his pretend paradise. Back into his long shirt, sweater, and ankle boots. Back in freezing Detroit.

But it didn't matter that he didn't actually go there. All Chris needed to do whenever he felt the urge to just switch off and relax, was simply close his eyes. He would always be able to find his remote islands. Its azure beach and warm weather. His paradise would forever wait for him.

The Secret Recipe

Duration: 60 minutes

Ever since she was a little girl, Simone was able to tell the difference between flavors. And I am not talking between the usual sweet and sour difference. No, I mean the really tricky taste. Like the difference between a peach and a nectarine. Her grandma would give her a slice of each, without the skin, and she would always be able to tell them apart. The trick was to look for the sweetness, which was more intense in nectarines. And if you think this isn't quite that big of a deal, keep in mind that she was only 3 at that time.

By the time she was five, she was helping her grandma in the kitchen. Not only to stir or add veggies, but also to unlock new flavors, play with ingredients, and even guess them. You see, the most memorable time about her helping out grandma in the kitchen was their little game – guess what. The point was for Simone to step out of the kitchen while her grandma added spices to the food. Then she would give her a taste – always a single teaspoon of the sauce – and Simone had to discover exactly which spices were added to the meal. She had always been a fan of curry powder, so that was usually the first thing she noticed whenever her grandma decided to add some. And every single time, whenever the word *Curry* would leave her mouth, a wide smile of content would appear.

Guess what, was something her grandma invented so she could keep Simone involved in the cooking process. But that wasn't the only reason why. Her grandma also wanted to strengthen the bond between the two of them, creating lasting memories that would keep Simone in love with cooking.

And she wasn't wrong. At the age of 25, Simone became the chef at one of the most prestigious restaurants in the city. She was not only well-recognized but also profoundly respected in the culinary world. She had worked alongside some of the most celebrated chefs and had gained many recognitions for her impressive skills, knowledge, and education.

She was still able to pinpoint exactly what spice, herb, or additive a meal has been enriched with, but there was still one thing she failed to do. And that was to figure out the secret ingredient in her grandma's cherry galette.

Her grandmother was a World War II survivor, and a French home cook who lost her husband while still young and managed to raise three boys all on her own. The fact that she had survived the war and was penniless for a decade, combined with her French heritage, meant that her kitchen offered a colorful menu. From finger-licking and incredibly cheap meals to real feasts for the pickiest tastes, there was a lot to learn from her cooking. Which was exactly was Simone did. If it wasn't for Nana, who knew where she would be today. It was her grandmother who did not only taught her anything there was to know, but she also rooted the culinary love deep within her, so when the time for choosing her education came, it was no choice, really. She always had known what she wanted to do for a living.

But, despite spending most of her childhood days with her grandma in the kitchen, there was still one thing she hadn't be able to learn. And that was the secret to making the rustic cherry galette.

You see, the fondest memory about cooking with her grandma was always the part when they made the desserts together. Her authentic madeleines, souffle, chocolate cake, even the best macaroons… Simone could copy every single dessert her grandma had ever made, except for one – the cherry galette.

When her grandmother passed away 10 years ago, Simone was the one who inherited all of her cookbooks and the collection of recipes that her grandma used to gather since she was a little girl. She had learned them all by heart, but none of them had the recipe for the cherry galette. She even turned her parents' house upside down, looking for a clue. She went through old newspapers, books, journals, all with the hope that she could find something, a piece of paper with the method, the ingredient list, something... But all was in wane. It had been 5 years since she started to search for the galette, and still, without hope.

The only thing she knew about the infamous cherry galette was that it was an old, authentic recipe that someone from a French pastry shop had given to her grandmother decades ago. And that was the only clue that she had to work with. She had been to Paris 4 times, and each time, it was a habit of hers to visit as many pastry shops as possible, trying out their galettes, hoping that he would find the one she had been looking for many years.

Now, as Simone was getting ready for her fifth visit in the city of light, she made a list of all the pastry shops that she should visit while there. It may seem easy to some. After all, how many pastry shops selling cherry galettes could there be in Paris. But, as it turned out, galettes were just as frequent as Macaroons, believe it or not. And since Paris was known to be the city of a thousand patisseries, you could only imagine the frustration and disappointment that followed after every bite. She literally had hundreds of cherry galettes to try and see if, hopefully, the bakery that had given the recipe to her grandmother was still active, and if, also, hopefully, they would still be selling it.

So she packed her grandmother's picture along with her other luggage and headed to the airport. This visit was supposed to be of a professional nature. She was invited to a culinary convention, and this was an excellent chance for her to gain some extra recognition for the restaurant she worked for. However, it didn't feel like that. It felt just like the previous four visits – as if she was heading to Paris with one goal and one goal only – to finally discover the secret to her grandmother's crispy and decadent cherry galette.

It was morning when Simone landed in Paris. Between the jet lag and the fact that she couldn't get a good shut-eye – she was always uncomfortable with sleeping near other people – Simone was feeling as if a train had run over her. She was so tired and utterly exhausted that the caffeine cravings made her feel cranky. Her initial plan was to go to the hotel, maybe try to get a couple of hours' sleep, and then start exploring Paris. And she would probably stay committed to this plan if the corner of her eye wasn't caught by something delicious from the tiny bakery at the airport. It was a galette. Although she couldn't tell if it was with cherries, strawberries, or other berries, she knew it was a sign for her to make a stop.

And that's what she did. And as it turned out, it was a galette with cherries. She knew that her grandma's authentic recipe couldn't possibly be discovered at the airport, but she had to give it a shot. And she was glad she did. Her gut was already rumbling, so the delicious galette combined with the intensity kick of the espresso was a decent treat. It wasn't the one she was looking for, but this galette was definitely worth trying.

A few hours later, when she finally woke up in her hotel, she was ready to go. The first stop was a well-known restaurant that she just had to check out. She had never been before, but since everybody had said that their French onion soup was the best in the world, she just had to taste it for herself. Under normal circumstances, she would fill her afternoon with fine wine, cheese, coq au vin, and top it off with some light Macaroons. But this was no ordinary day. She had work to do. Her grandma's galette was hiding somewhere in this charming city, and she wasn't to give up that easy.

To anyone else, this would seem like a waste of time. But not to Simone. You see, it wasn't just because she could still feel the taste of the sweet galette, the sour cherries lingering well after the bite had been swallowed. It wasn't just about the pure decadence – although that alone would be worth it. It wasn't entirely about reconnecting with her late grandma either, they had a special bond, after all. It was mainly because this was the only thing about her grandma's cooking that she hadn't managed to crack yet. She had made hundreds of galettes ever since her grandmother had passed, but none of it was quite like the real thing. They all tasted great, Simone was an extraordinary chef, after all, but her grandma's recipe remained a mystery. And mysteries were there to be solved.

The taste was there, it was almost like she could taste it, even though it had been more than a decade since she last had a piece of the cherry delight. So it was no doubt that she would be able to detect it right away. If only she could find it.

The French soup was all that Simone had hoped for. And even though she was tempted to try every single dish on the menu, she had no time to waste. She had many sugary treats reserved for the afternoon.

The first stop was a little patisserie just around the corner, so it was the obvious starting point for her galette adventure. Unfortunately, but also surprisingly, they sold no galettes. There was a wide array of Tarte Tatins presented, but not a single galette.

The next stop was a bakery that was about a 3-minute walk away. Her eyes sparkled when she noticed the cherries on top of what seemed to look like the crispest pastry. The owner was an older lady who was also selling her cakes. Simone told her story and explained her journey, and the lady was kind enough to give her a generous bite of the pie, without charging anything. Simone knew that she would have many galettes to try, so she was only eating one bite of each.

Unfortunately, this wasn't the one she was looking for. After thanking the lady and complimenting on the amazing taste of the cherry pie, Simone was on her way again.

She had tried a dozen of galettes when she started to lose all hope. She was getting tired, and even though she deeply enjoyed her tasting galette adventure, there were clearly many other things a chef like herself could do in Paris. She committed to only a few more tries, and then she promised herself she would embark on a real culinary exploration.

The next pastry shop she visited had been around for over 100 years. The woman who worked there explained to Simone that she was a relatively new employee, but that the founder's grandson would be there shortly if she wanted to wait for him and maybe have a chat. Simone knew that she didn't have the time, and just as she was getting ready to politely refuse, a man walked in.

"Oh, here is Monsieur Bernard," the seller said, pointing her head at the man who had just walked in.

Then, a conversation in French followed, but besides *woman* and *galette*, Simone couldn't decipher what the two of them were saying. She used to learn French for a couple of years in school, but clearly, she was out of practice.

The man greeted Simone and invited her to sit in one of the small, secluded tables at the end of the pastry shop.

"I hear that you are wishing to recreate an old recipe. What is it, a galette?" the man asked.

Surprised at his great English accent, Simone answered, "Yes. My grandmother was from France, and she was a great cook. Although self-taught, she passed her passion and cooking skills to me. That's why I decided to take that path and become a chef. So you can see how frustrating this can be for me. I've worked alongside the greatest chefs of today, and yet, I still haven't been able to crack the mystery and find the secret ingredient of her cherry galette."

"I am sorry for asking, but why is this so important for you" the man asked.

"Well, I am not sure how I can explain it, really. I guess I am not sure myself. But the truth is, I was able to find every single recipe my grandmother had made. She was an avid cook and a recipe collector, so everything she had ever made – no matter how insignificant - was always written down in one of her recipe books. But I haven't been able to find anything about the galette, and that somehow bothers me. It is not a pride thing, it is not that I haven't been able to decipher the taste. I don't know, I just think that there's more to the story here." Simone explained, unsure whether this would make any sense to the man or not.

"My grandma Josephine told me how she would come to this pastry shop every day when she was a kid, and that she always shared a cherry galette with her friend there. I guess it also has sentimental value to me," she said, showing the framed picture of her grandma to the man.

The man nodded and asked the woman to bring them a slice of the galette and a cup of coffee.

Somehow, Simone had a strange feeling about this. Could this be the place? Was she really going to end her pursuit and find what she was looking for all along? Just as she was starting to get excited, the woman served them what the man had asked for. All of the excitement disappeared once Simone discovered that the galette was not made with cherries, but raspberries.

"I am sorry. I would gladly try your galette, as I am sure it is very delicious. However, I don't think this is the recipe that I have been looking for. My grandma used to make cherry galettes." Simone said, unable to hide the disappointment on her face.

The man smiled and told her to just try it. So Simone listened. As soon as she sank her teeth into the pie, a familiar flavor hit her taste buds. Suddenly, she was not in the small bakery in Paris, but in her grandma's farmhouse, enjoying a dessert in the kitchen.

"But how is this possible? How did you know that this was the recipe I was looking for. Clearly, these are raspberries. I can taste the difference in flavor here, but the pastry is exactly the same. There is also the familiar sourness, although not so intense as these are raspberries. But there is no doubt that this is the recipe. How is this possible?" Simone just couldn't hide the shock and content that danced together all over her face.

"It *was* a cherry galette. We tweaked the recipe about 5-6 years ago. Tourists prefer our cherry tart tatin, you see, so we needed to offer variety and decided to replace the cherries from the galette with raspberries. The taste, as you can notice, is quite similar, so I guess no crime was made. At least I hope that my grandfather would approve if he were here with us today," the man said.

"But that wasn't why I was certain that this was the galette you were looking for. It was the picture. I recognized it right away. If you could wait here for a few minutes, I will explain it all." The man told Simone, while jumping from his seat.

Simone was even more shocked, but of course that she agreed. How could this man know something of her grandma that she wasn't aware of?

The man headed upstairs. As it turned out, that's where he lived. This was a family patisserie for three generations now. And all three generations had lived in the apartment above.

When he finally came down, about five minutes later, the man carried a small box with him. He put it on the table and opened its lock to deliver the contents. The first thing that he showed her was the exact same picture that Simone was holding in her hands.

"I believe that this is your grandmother," he said, turning the picture over. "To Jean-Andre, thank you for our time together. We part ways, but you will always remain in my heart. Love, Josephine".

Simone remained in shock. She came here to find a simple recipe but discovered so much more about her grandmother's life.

"My grandfather would always speak fondly of your grandma. She was the love of his life. They spent years together. As I remember, she lived nearby, so they were close since they were kids. He met my grandmother 2 years after your grandma had moved to America, and well, life did the rest."

She couldn't believe. He knew the story of how her grandmother moved to the USA about 10 years after the war. She had met her grandfather a few years later and shortly gave birth to her uncle. But she knew nothing of her old life in Paris.

"But that's not all. The cherry galette was something that your grandma and my grandpa invented together," the man said, showing her a picture of the two of them together as kids, with the galette recipe written on the other side.

A déjà vu hit Simone. She knew this picture. She had seen it before. But she was certain that it was nowhere to be found among her grandma's things. And then it struck her. She opened the frame, and sure enough, the picture was there. Josephine and

Jean-Andre as kids. She turned the picture over, and there it was – the recipe for the cherry galette. She was chasing it all of these years, while the answer was always on her bedside table. Hidden from the rest of the world. Forever kept a secret.

"I guess there are some things that are best not shared with the rest of the world. Some things that are so dear to your heart, that telling them to another soul would feel like a betrayal. I understand it now. Although I cannot lie that I am happy to have discovered the truth and found the recipe," Simone said, tracing her fingertips across the old photograph.

Farewell, City Lights!

Duration: 65 minutes

To Will, London was everything. It was the place he grew up in, where he was born. He knew every corner, every street like the back of his hand. He didn't only live in London – he lived there while loving the city with all of his heart. And he would also love to think that Lonon loved him back.

How could he not think that? He had managed to find his dream job after the very first interview he ever went to. He managed to win over the most beautiful girl he had ever seen, with a single look. He was charming, but not that lucky, surely. He thought of his city as this magical place when nothing bad had ever happened to him. Love something deeply, and the strong emotion will surely be returned. That was his motto.

But right now, as he was getting ready for the new and most important chapter of his life, all of a sudden, London started to seem less friendly. The streets he once walked with comfort and feelings of security were now these terrible places where you could be robbed or hit by a car. The chatter that lulled him to sleep late at night when he would open the window to let the city air in, now seemed annoying and disorienting. His job, as much as he loved it, had also started to feel meaningless. Not profound enough, not rooted in something of vital importance.

The city was a real beauty, but at the same time, it was no place for raising a beautiful daughter. Everything seemed shallow. As if somehow everyone had lost their values overnight. It was all peaceful and safe until he took Emma in his hands for the very first time. When her little baby eyes locked his, it was like seeing daylight for the first time. Everything seemed clearer. And everything he once thought to be important seemed to be fading away.

It was surely a feeling that every father in the world shared. It was impossible not to feel protective of your little bundle of love, but this felt more than just him trying to keep his daughter from harm. It also felt like a wake-up call. He was feeling as though he was asleep for a very long time. Like he was just waking up from a long coma, and somehow, the whole world had changed. He knew that he had to turn his whole life around. Not just because of the arrival of his daughter. But also because he had just realized that he needed deeper connections and a real purpose.

But there was something that was bothering him. He wasn't quite sure that his wife, Rose, shared the same feelings, as he knew how much Rose loved the city life, as well. The busy streets, the late-night eating, the lifestyle on the fast lane. She was a real city girl, and she feared that she would not agree with him that finding a more peaceful place to raise their children would be a wise decision.

So he said nothing. After all, Rose had just given birth to Emma. Clearly, this talk would require clearer head and undisturbed emotions. He decided to wait for a better time. He would give their life a shot for 6 months, or even a year, and then see where London would lead them to. Besides, he thought, maybe this was just something he felt at the spur of the moment. The adrenaline kicked in, the fatherly instincts took over, and he felt differently. But, maybe, once he gave himself the time to cool off, he would not share the same feelings.

And that's what he did. It had been five months since Emma was born, and Will hadn't said a single word about his concerns regarding the city life to Rose. And even though he sincerely hoped that the things that bothered him would disappear, he still felt the same. In fact, these disturbing feelings grew more intense with each day that passed. Every time that they would go out for a walk, he would be reminded of how easy it would be for the city to just swallow, chew up, and then spit them out, leaving them wounded and scarred for life.

As they were strolling down their street, he couldn't take his eyes of his daughter. He was thinking about how pure and fragile this beautiful little creature was. He wanted to magically keep her in a safety bubble where she would forever keep her innocence. Away from things that could hurt her, away from the rest of the world.

Will wasn't delusional, though. He knew that, even if they went to live at the end of the world, the reality would hit Emma at some point. No matter how hard he would try to keep her safe, he was aware that the time would come when she would be ready to explore the world on her own. Make her own choices, learn from her own mistakes.

But he was also well aware that for every harsh thing in the world, there was also something beautiful to be found. He believed that there was purity and simplicity to be discovered. Something that would help them shape their daughter into a kind, honest, and, most importantly, a good person. Someone that would know the real values. And the only way to achieve that, he thought, was to move away from the stressful city life.

So Will thought it was time to bite the bullet and talk to Rose about it. Back home, as she was preparing their dinner, he told her that there was something that he would like to discuss with her. She was impatient to know what that was about at first, but Will had explained to her that it would be best if they discussed it once they feed and put Emma to sleep. She agreed as it was obvious that Will had something important to talk to her about, and she also didn't want to be disrupted.

Once Ema was soundly asleep, they sat in their living room, opened a bottle of wine, and started their life-changing talk.

"I have given this quite a lot of thought, so please, hear what I have to say first, before deciding against it," Will started. Then he spent a good twenty minutes talking about how the city was no place to raise kids, how they would never be free enough to do the things they want to do, how they would never be able to enjoy life while they were working from 9 to 5, sometimes even on the weekends... "We will just never find the time to raise her the way I think a kid should be raised. With love, patience, and most importantly, freedom. You see how these kids live now. You have to schedule playdates for them to play with each other. Isn't that crazy? Why would we want to be slaves to this busy lifestyle? Why not take it slow and enjoy each milestone together, without stressing over things that, at the end of the day, aren't really important to us," he said, waiting for her response.

He feared the worst – for Rose to say that the city is full of opportunities, or even worse, to tell him that this was a new phase in his life so he was getting confused – didn't quite know what he was talking about.

But, to his surprise, she did the exact opposite. "You do not know this, but I've silently given it a lot of thought, as well. This may come as a surprise to you, that me, the forever-in-love-with-the-city girl would consider moving to the countryside. But that is exactly what I have been dreaming about this past couple of months. Just us in a cottage somewhere. Living sustainably, being in touch with nature, teaching Emma the real values in life. I guess having a kid just changes your whole perspective," Rose said while shooting him a teary-eyed look.

Will couldn't believe what he was hearing. He immediately jumped from his seat and gave Rose a hug so tight that she could barely breathe. Then they spent the whole evening talking about how this new life of theirs would feel, about how they would be able to grow their own food, eat organic eggs, have a dozen pets. They both agree that this was not only the best thing for Emma but for them, as well. They had been suffocating in the city for so long that they really needed a change—a chance to be free and breathe life in at full capacity.

Since it was a weekend, they stayed up really late, talking, fantasizing, planning. One would think that they would spend the next morning in bed, but no, Rose was actually up before Emma. In fact, she wasn't sure if she had gotten any sleep, either. It all felt surreal somewhat. Like a dream. Were they really serious? Were they even up for the challenge? Wanting something is one thing, but being able to actually see it through is something else entirely. And the truth was, neither Will nor Rose had any experience in country living. Nor knew a thing about livestock. And besides the half-dead plant that stood by their window, they haven't even grown a thing together.

The more she was thinking about it, the stronger the panic grew. What if they changed their mind too late? What if they were to find out that they were not cut out for being homesteaders the hard way? What if they were to sell their apartment and purchase a cottage that no one would even want to buy? How would they return back to London? Where would they leave then?

Just as she was starting to let anxiety completely consume her thoughts, Will gave her a kiss on the cheek. He always knew just how to calm her down and instill reassurance. "We have some planning to do," he said.

Rose, then, told him of her concerns and how she was scared to start such a different chapter in their life – one that they knew nothing about. She also explained to him that she didn't quite believe that they would master such a different life easily, but she also admitted that she still believed that it was something that they needed to do. For Emma's, but also for their sake as well.

"That is what's most important, don't you think? We don't need a manual or someone to instruct us how we should make the transition. We will learn on the go. After all, isn't it always best to learn from your own mistakes? I am not delusional, though, I don't think it will be a walk in the park. It will most likely be hard, especially at first. Making such a transition is never easy. But if it is something that we are absolutely sure we want, and if we are together and love each other, well, I really think that there is nothing in the world that can stop us from succeeding." Will explained, giving her a look that screamed excitement.

That was exactly what Rose needed at this moment. For him to drag her back to her safety zone – to tell her that everything was going to be alright. To reassure her that with love and some effort, anything was possible. She smiled back and returned the kiss – "Let's do it," she finally agreed.

They spent the whole day looking for the perfect place they would be happy to move to. There were quite a few options that were worth considering, but they both agreed that they were mostly charmed with a small village that they had once passed through. Even then, it seemed magical to them. Although they hadn't admitted it, they always envied people who lived at a slower pace, without all the stress and busy obligations that were inevitable when living in the city.

So they began their hunt for houses. Both Will and Rose agreed that they didn't just want a 3-bedroom cottage, but they also wanted to own a big piece of land. They wanted to live in an authentic farmhouse – somewhere they can cultivate their food, raise livestock, and live sustainably.

Just when Will thought that, having such particular requirements and finding them in such a small area was almost impossible, an ad caught their eyes. It was the cutest farmhouse they had ever laid their eyes on. It had four bedrooms, two bathrooms, and a large open-concept kitchen and living room. Plus, there was a laundry room situated near the backdoor, so Rose was thrilled about the idea of updating it a little bit and turning it into a mudroom as well. They would need one after all if they were to become proper farmers.

They knew they had no time to waste, so Will made the call almost instantly. The real estate agent explained to them that the people were still living in the house, and were scheduled to move the next month. She also said that if they wanted to go and take a look, she would love to speak to the owners first and schedule an appropriate time. Will and Rose agreed. All they had to do now was wait for the agent to call them back with the news.

Half an hour later, the lady called. She told them that there would always be someone at the house, as the owners were packing and planning their move. They had told her that the house would be open for visitors during an appropriate time. So 9-5 worked well for them.

That meant that Will and Rose could go and have a look at the house the next day. They called to let the owners know that they would be arriving just before noon the next day. It was a 4-hour drive, so they had the return trip to consider, as well. They were planning on bringing Emma, so it was important for them to stick to a healthy timetable that worked for them all.

It was 7 AM the next day when they started their trip. Nor Will neither Rose said much during the drive, as they were both silently obsessing over details in their mind. Would the owners accept their offer? Would they even like the house? Then a stream of thoughts of them leading the homesteading life took over, just to remind them why they were doing this in the first place.

Four hours later, when they finally arrived at the place, there were reassured that this was the decision of their life. The place was the most peaceful spot on earth that they had ever seen. It truly looked like it was crafted out of a fairytale. The greenery was almost surreal, and they were amazed at how lush the grass was there. And the cottages? They were the most charming pieces of architecture. Unlike anything they had seen in London.

They thought that they would have trouble finding the place, but they were so wrong. It almost looked like it was the place that had found them. A large gate surrounded by huge trees on both sides opened up to a long driveway that led to the house of their dreams. When they got to the house, they both realized that it was actually more charming than how it looked in the photos. There was land on both sides of the house, but the biggest piece was situated behind.

The owners were a charming older couple, probably in their 60s. They greeted them with a smile on their face, glad to see that a young family was interested in moving to the countryside. They had spent all of their life there, and now, with their kids being gone, they just wanted something simpler. It was getting hard for them to manage the property, and, as the man was honest to say, they needed a breather. They had told them how the farmhouse was bought and restored by them 30 years ago – it was actually built in the 30s.

Inside, the place had such a warmth that neither Will nor Rose had been lucky enough to experience. They both had grown up in large city apartments, so this was all new to them. They went through the house carefully, inspecting every corner, although they really didn't need to. It had won them over as soon as the door was opened.

They got out through the back door. After the owner ended showing them how far their land spread, they sat at a wooden table in their backyard to discuss things further. Will didn't want to waste any more time. He and Rose both nodded in approval (their secret sign) when they were still inside, so that meant that it was time to get serious. Serious about moving to the countryside. Serious about buying this particular house. So, Will got to the point. He explained to the owners why they had decided to make such a change. Rose added that they fell in love with the house as soon as they had laid eyes on it, and that they would be thrilled to, someday, call it their home.

Will, then, showed the owners their offer. They spend a minute in silence while the owners shared a look. Then, the man said: "To be honest, I am just happy that we are selling the house to a young and loving family such as yourself. We bought this house when our kids were very little, so we understand the importance of moving from the superficial and trying to teach lasting values to your children. We had already done that. And we are glad. We just think it is time for us to move on to something simpler. You know, we had spent most of our lives here. Now that it is just the two of us, we would like to have adventures of our own. Travel, explore, see the world, that sort of things. What I am trying to say is, we are in a little bit of hurry to make the sale. Your offer seems more than fair, so, yes, we gladly accept it."

Rose and Will couldn't hide their happiness. And just as Rose was telling them all about her wishes and ideas for the place, asking gardening questions, and soaking in every piece of advice she was given, Will was already on the phone with the real estate agent, telling her the good news.

They spent another hour with the owners, learning as much as possible about this place, the house, the overall lifestyle. When the time came for them to head back to London, they started to feel sad, all of a sudden. They were already beginning to miss this place. That is how close to their hearts, it immediately rooted itself.

As they were driving away, they couldn't help but look at their daughter. Imagining her in this peacefulness, running around freely, playing outside – something they would never have in the city. At that moment, Will squeezed Rose's hand tightly. They didn't have to say a word. The look they shared was enough. Enough for them to know this was the right decision. Enough to make the life-altering transition that would bring freedom and calmness into their lives.

The 18th Century Beauty

Duration: 30 minutes

For three centuries, this place had looked the same. Its stone exterior was probably polished and washed a dozen times, but overall, the structure had remained unchanged. If the stones could talk, they would have some extraordinary stories to tell. The house, being around since the early 18th century, had endured wars and changes that no one could even imagine. It had been a home for many generations, providing shelter and security for its residents.

It had an undeniable charm – something that you couldn't find in a newer build. A curb appeal that you didn't need to work hard on – it was simply there. You didn't need to hire a professional to help you with the design, nor you needed to buy fancy things to make it charming. The house didn't need beautifying, it oozed authenticity and timeless elegance. All it needed was some love, and the century-old beauty that was hidden behind the wrinkles of time would come out on its own.

Perhaps that's why Sean had always been drawn to it. Because you didn't have to pretend. You didn't need to make it something it was not. There would never be anything fake about this house. There was a lot of pretend going around these days. Faux beams, wooden-like tiles, stone-like stickers that tricked your mind into thinking you were looking at the real deal… He had seen quite a lot of those in his career.

Since the day that Sean had officially started working as an architect, he had one goal in mind – find a real gem and restore its original beauty. You would think that, having architecture in his heart, he would want to build his dream house from scratch, make it his own sanctuary. Work on every single corner so that he would be sure that the house would fit his every need and desire. But there was something about these old builds that drew Sean's attention like a magnet. Calling him to reveal their ancient story. Begging him to preserve the century-old beauty.

And this house was the diamond in the rough that Sean was looking for all along. Although, in all fairness, he didn't exactly find it. He knew about this house since he was a little kid. Sean grew up in this neighborhood. And, as a kid, every day, he would walk to school and pass through this street, walking past this stone house. He remembered that, at one time, there was a family of five living here. The kids were a few years older than him, so they were never really friends. He knew the name of the youngest boy,

Tim, as they had played basketball together a few times, but that was it. He was never close to him enough to get invited inside. This was the first time that Sean was to step inside the old stone house that stood around the corner for three long centuries.

The stone house had been vacant for 5 years now. It had been on the market for almost 3 months, To Sean's luck, people preferred newer buildings. Besides, there wasn't that many people thrilled to spend that asking price just for the sake of the charm and the incredible stories that these walls had seen. But to Sean, the charm was all worth it. Why would you even want to buy a house in the first place, he thought. Anyone could get some bricks, wood, or stones, and make a wall. The ones that had the privilege to live inside walls that have stood for hundreds of years, however, were quite rare. And he wanted to be a part of the latter so badly.

He knew that the house was too big for him. Really, all he needed was a small kitchen, a living room, a bathroom, and a decent bedroom with a comfortable bed. He was living alone, after all. But, unlike his colleagues and friends, he didn't share the same feelings. He was always one to plan things ahead, calculate losses before they had even occurred, get prepared for unexpected situations… And this was no different. He didn't want to buy a house and have to sell it in a couple of years when he would decide on forming a family. No, he wanted a place he would call home. A place where he and his future wife would raise their children. Someplace they would have comfort. A house where they could be happy. And he had no doubt that this stone house could give that (and more) to anyone who decided to live there.

The purchase hadn't be sealed yet. After all, Sean had yet to look inside the house, but he had no doubt that he would be amazed at the condition the house was in. If he was to judge by looking at the exterior, he would say that it was in great shape.

When the real estate agent finally showed up to unlock the door – Sean did arrive a little bit earlier – he realized that the house was even more beautiful on the inside than on the outside. A giant fireplace greeted him as soon as he walked inside – it was the first thing one could notice straight from the door. And it was the grandest thing about the place, either. Situated in the large family room, Sean instantly imagined it bringing warmth and comfort to generation after generation. He imagined families sitting cozily in a cold winter afternoon, sharing stories, laughing, enjoying life. He even imagined Tim and his family there. He only wished that this house could provide such comfort for him, as well.

The kitchen was spacious, and the large window above the sink offered a view into the backyard. The yard wasn't particularly big, and it was not well-maintained, but it didn't need much, either. Sean was aware that there had not been any residents here for 5 years, so an occasional mowing here and there was all love that this house had been getting these past few years. Of course, that was all about to change once he planted his roots there. He would do his best to maintain and take care of this house until its original charm wasn't completely restored.

Upstairs, there were three large bedrooms, one of which – the master one, he assumed – had the potential to be divided so an extra room could be gained, if the need for that was ever to arise. There were two bathrooms upstairs and one half-bath downstairs, which Sean thought was perfect.

The house was freshly painted, the hardwood floors were in excellent shape, and the tiles in the bathroom had been recently replaced. The only thing he had to do at this point was to just move all of his things inside and start a new chapter in this ancient stone house.

He was certain that this was everything he had ever wanted, so he made the offer. He waited a day, two, three… Still, there was no sign. The offer was below the asking price, surely, but who in the right mind offers the actual price? You always bid below and then agree on something in between – something that neither side will be thrilled about, but both satisfied enough to accept it.

The real estate agent had told him that he would hear from him within 48 hours, and yet, three days had passed without a sign. Just as he was getting ready to call and see for himself, his phone rang. It was him.

He was getting prepared for a disappointment – a refusal that would shatter his fantasy about living in the stone house he grew up admiring. Or at least, he would be asked to increase the offered price. To his surprise, neither of that happened. Instead, the real estate agent had called him to say that the owner is in a bit of a hurry, and as eager as they are to sell the house, they are okay with his offer. Therefore, all there is left for them to do is sign the contract and seal the deal.

Two months had passed, and Sean was carrying his boxes inside. He arranged the furniture in a way that suited his bachelor needs, although he was sure that, when the time would come, there would be plenty of room and potential for making this place warm and family-like home.

Just as he was unpacking his last box and putting his books on the shelf near the window, he shot a look outside just to be transported back in time. A kid, no more than 9 years old, was passing through with his school bag on his back. Their eyes locked, and he couldn't help but notice how impressed the kid was with the house. Or did he just imagine it? It didn't matter really, as for a second there, he wasn't the grown-up Sean who was living in the stone house. He was the third-graded passing through, admiring the people who lived in such a grand and ancient building. And who knew? Perhaps the kid would also grow up to buy this house from him, keeping the tradition alive, making sure that the stone house forever stayed loved and taken care of.

Chasing a Dream

Duration: 55 minutes

For as long as she could remember, Mary had vivid dreams. And these were not your ordinary dreams that would sometimes be colored into the most vibrant colors ever seen. No, this was something else entirely. At night, when she would fall asleep, it felt as though she came alive in her dreams. Almost like she was never really sleeping.

When she was young, her mother used to tell her that we were never unconscious when sleeping. It was just how others perceived us. "We simply step into another world, is all. Another dimension that can be reached only deep in your mind, once you detach yourself from the things that surround you – once you let go of reality. You will then slowly start your trip to this place. And once you get there, anything is possible. You can be whoever and whatever you want to be. There are no right or wrong choices there. No one is there to judge you or correct your moves. You don't need to be human at all, if you don't want to be. You can choose to be a bird, flying freely in the sky, reaching far destinations, seeing anything from above. Or you can be a tree – standing tall on the ground, playing games with the wind, allowing the sun to warm you up all they long. Or you can be a river. Endlessly flowing in a beautiful stream, giving home to small fish, providing life. It doesn't matter what you choose there, because you cannot be wrong," she would say.

And that was what Mary did. She used to let her dreams consume her completely, giving all of her energy to them, allowing them to just swallow her up so she could spend some time into her magical dreamland – the place she had created only for herself. People would say that your dreams are not something that could be controlled, but Mary always liked to think otherwise. To her, she was the creator of her dreams. They were not conscious decisions, something she would construct while awake, but rather series of moves and choices that her sub-conscious would make for her. But what was the sub-conscious if not a part of her?

She always believed that our sub-conscious is something that we feed slowly and gradually. Like a large pot or container where you would simply put stuff that you don't want to think about at the moment. Like your unfinished obligations, fears, desires, fantasies. Whatever it was that we had strong feelings about belonged in that container. And all of us, every single person, did that. We all filled the containers without even knowing it. At least that was her theory of how dreams happen.

Nevertheless, she had always vivid imagination and exciting dreams. And nothing seemed to surprise her. Whether she was riding a Pegasus or sitting as a tulip in a field full of lilies, Mary was used to playing a part in her excentric dream stories. That is why she was surprised to be feeling this way today.

Last night was different. She couldn't remember if she had ever felt like this about a dream she had. Surely, her dreams would leave her confused at times, but not like this. This dream had a completely different vibe. Strange, unfamiliar, somewhat worrying. Why did she feel this way? After all, it wasn't such a weird dream at all. Perhaps it was that? Could she be so used to entering a strange world at night, that she found anything less eccentric to be worrying?

It started with a place that was well-known to her. A place that she frequently visited with her mother when she was a kid. It was a place on the beach, just a half-hour drive away from her childhood home. She hadn't bee there in ages, not since they moved when she was still young, anyway.

Her dream started with that place. She was alone, lying on the beach, enjoying the warm weather. Then, all of a sudden, she stood up and decided to jump into the water. She kept swimming and swimming and swimming until she could barely see the beach. She had never been able to go this deep. It felt good, liberating somehow. She spent some time enjoying the sun on her face there, and then decided to swim back. When she got out of the water, she didn't feel tired at all. She didn't even need to pat her skin dry. She just kept on going. She seemed certain of her direction like she knew where she was going. Like there was something familiar hiding behind the lush trees– something she had seen before.

She was making slow steps, calmly walking towards the place. She knew exactly where to go. The pathway, although it couldn't be seen from the beach, was something she found immediately – she knew where it was. Once she entered the forest, nothing seemed extraordinary or out of place there— just trees, butterflies, and thick grass everywhere. But she didn't stop – she hadn't reached her destination yet. And so she kept on going and going, step by step by step. Time was tricky to track in her dreams, so she couldn't possibly tell how long it took her to get from the beach to the place she was looking for. A few minutes, 15, half an hour? She couldn't be sure. Once she got there, even in her dream, it seemed that she had found peace. She sat on the only bench that was there and enjoyed the view.

All around the bench, there were flowers. All divided into color groups, this colorful view spread as far as the eye could see. On the left, there were white flowers, then yellow, orange, red, pink, purple… But these weren't flowers of the same kind. It looked as though that every known flower that was white was planted there. So was the case with the yellow, orange, reg, pink, and purple flowers. So many different colors in so many vibrant colors.

Mary stayed seated on the beach for quite some time. Again, it wasn't sure just how long. One thing was certain, though, she enjoyed the sight in front of her, deeply. It wasn't just the colorful view that seemed heavenly there. The flowery scent combined with the gentle breeze was so peaceful and comforting, that Mary didn't want to get up and leave. And so decided to stay there, tilt her head back, and just enjoy herself. Then, she closed her eyes and settled into a fetal position on the bench. It was almost like she could hear herself breathing deeply and gently. In and out. In and out. In and out.

And that was it. Mary woke up after that, feeling confused about her dream. First, she had never watched herself relax and fall asleep in a dream – never. Then, there was also the familiar place which was combined with the flowery paradise, which somehow felt odd to her. But as she was used to dreaming all sorts of weird things, she quickly shrugged it off.

She thought about the dream when she was getting ready for bed that night but didn't really give it that much thought, as Mary knew that, once her eyes were closed, she would find her eccentric world again.

But that didn't happen. For some strange reason, Mary had the exact same dream again. It started the same, with her swimming and swimming for as far as she could go, then returning to the beach and starting to walk toward the place with thousands of flowers. Just like the previous night, Mary also sat on the bench, enjoyed the sight, tilted her head back, and then finally, lied down and started breathing slowly and gently until she was lulled to sleep.

Although she started to get a strange sensation, Mary also tried to find reason in this odd situation. To her, the only logical explanation would be that yesterday, she was so affected by this dream, that she somehow recreated it again. But, to the very last detail? It all felt too unusual, so she decided not to think about it again.

And she probably wouldn't if she wasn't revisited by the same dream. Third night in a row, Mary dreamt of the beach she knew too well. She dreamt of her swimming far, then coming back to the shore again. She dreamt of her walking and walking down an unknown, but somehow, familiar path. She saw herself enjoying the sight of thousands and thousands of colorful flowers while sitting on the only bench in the forest. Again, she tilted her head back and then simply fell asleep in a comfortable position while breathing slowly.

Surely this couldn't be a coincidence. Nor was she able to recreate the same dream down to the tiniest detail for the third time in a row. As strange as her dreams could get, this felt creepy. Why was she dreaming of this place? Was this place even real? Surely she would remember if she had ever seen so many flowers clumped together in such a weird way? Or maybe he simply forgot. There was one way to find out, and that was to ask her mother.

Mary took her phone and rang. She didn't want to worry her mother and tell her that she had been dreaming such a vivid dream for three nights in a row. After all, she knew how her she was about these things. She would force her into the car and forced her to drive and see if this place had existed. And she was the type of woman who just had to put meaning even behind the most insignificant of things.

When she finally answered, after the fifth or sixth ring, they spend a couple of minutes talking about the weather, Mary's work, an old recipe. Mary didn't want to just jump straight to the question as her mother would sense that something was bothering her. Instead, she played it as cool as she knew how. Once she realized the air was clear for dropping that bomb, she said, "Have we ever been to a place with a lot of flowers when I was a kid? Someplace near the beach where we spent our weekends?".

"Not that I recall," her mother answered. "Why?"

"No reason, I guess I just miss the beach since this cold weather had started. I had a vague memory of us sitting and observing a bunch of flowers, but it could have been just a dream. Forget about it." Mary said, trying to sound as undisturbed as possible. "Or maybe because I have some work to finish tomorrow in a place nearby, maybe I got sentimental."

That was a lie. She had no business nowhere near their old home or that beach. But just now, in the spur of the moment, Mary decided that she wouldn't be able to sit still or think about anything else than that place unless she went there and checked it out. Could that place really exist?

It was still morning, and she had almost 5 hours of driving, so she decided to speed things up. She packed a small bag for a one-night stay, grabbed her essentials, and headed out.

During her long drive, she couldn't help but think whether she was crazy for doing this. Was she really chasing something that she had seen in her dream? Clearly, that was irrational behavior. What was she really hoping to find there? All types of flowers categorized by color? And how could such a long field of flowers be placed within a secluded part of the woods? As the hours passed she became less and less certain of her decision. It was too late to turn around and go home now – she would have to see this through.

But, she also couldn't help to notice that, despite her thoughts of irrationality and, well, pure craziness, that wasn't the only thing she worried about. In fact, she didn't worry that she went on this strange adventure. The thing she was worried was – what if this place really existed? What if she really found this bench and these colorful flowers there? What would that mean?

Five hours had passed when she arrived at her destination. She parked her car near the beach, grabbed her bag, and headed down. There was a young couple holding hands in the distance, but other than them, there was not a living soul on the beach. She didn't expect to find anyone, really. The weather was too cold for the beach.

She looked around to make sure that no one was looking at her. She didn't want to look like a lost or crazy person trying to find a way to enter the woods. But the truth was, she didn't even have to try. Because, as it turned out, the entry was there. Just where she entered in her dream, the pathway started at that exact spot. She didn't have to look for it, either; her dream was clear. All she had to do was find the giant rock and then turn right. And the path was there.

If you didn't know where to look, it was pretty impossible to detect it from the beach. Covered by a rock and large trees, no one would suspect that you could enter the woods from there.

She looked around again, and when she was sure that the couple was not able to see her, she stepped inside. The pathway looked exactly like it did in her dream, although she wasn't sure whether that surprised or terrified her at this moment. Would she really find flowers there? What if there was something else? She stopped for a second, unsure whether she should keep going forward. Was it safer to just leave? She gave it a quick thought but soon discarded that option. She didn't come this far only to turn around. She had to see.

The pathway was as long as it was in her dream. She checked her phone and realized that she had been walking for 5 minutes, and still, no sign of the flowery paradise. But there was nowhere to go but forward now. So, step by step, she kept on moving until five more minutes had passed, and she found her mind completely blown away. White, yellow, orange, red, pink, and purple flowers of all sorts spread on a large field in front of her. The bench was not as it was in her dream, but it was placed on the same spot. Which told her only one thing – she had been here before. She didn't remember when, she had no idea who she was with, but one thing was certain – she had definitely been here before.

She sat on the bench, admiring the sight before her. She had to take a dozen pictures to memorize this. Not only because the sight was so beautiful, it was hard to resist not to capture it, but in case another dream appeared. That way, she would have something to compare it to.

As she was observing the beauty that surrounded here, it suddenly hit her. What if she had come here with her late father? She would like to think that her father was watching her from above, visiting her in her dreams. This was his way of telling her to take a breath, and literally, stop to smell the roses. There are beautiful things in life to be discovered and seen. We all need to just hit the pause button sometimes and simply let life in.

The Silver Notebook

Duration: 60 minutes

Mark pulled the car in the driveway, but somehow, he couldn't muster the strength to get out of it. He was standing in front of his childhood home. The place where he was born and spent the first half of his life. The place that offered warmth and shelter for so many years. The place where his mather would always greet him with a warm meal and a fresh pie. Even after so many years. Whenever he would come and visit, he would always find her in the kitchen, preparing his favorite dishes, making sure that her little boy was satisfied.

She lived in an apartment in the city now. It was easier that way for everyone. Since his father had passed away last year, it got pretty hard, not to mention, lonely, for her to be managing the house all by herself. He knew that she would be happier in the city, where they would be able to spend more time together, where she would be with her grandchildren every day. And that's what they did. A couple of months ago, his 67-year old mother moved to an apartment that was just a 10-minute walk away from them. Even though she was living alone, she never felt lonely. And just the thought of them being so close to each other was comforting. It was a good decision for everyone. That way, he and his wife could have someone to be with their children when needed, and her mother was thrilled to be spending quality time with them regularly.

So, it was understandable why he couldn't find the strength to get inside the house now. The house that was always filled with laughter and love, now stood empty and cold. It was heartbreaking, really. Not only because his father was gone, but also because he would never be able to sleep in his old room again. Nor would he be able to teach his son Dave how to throw a ball in the backyard, the way his father had taught him. There would be no Christmases under the big tree there, no holidays to celebrate—no fighting over the remote. There will be no yelling over who had eaten the last piece of cake. All these insignificant little things now seemed as important as anything else in life.

He was on the verge of shedding a tear when his phone rang – it was his mother. She had called to ask him if he could go through his parents' bedroom once again, as she was sure she had forgotten something in the drawer there. She just wanted to remind him that that was a place he should check, as well. Because that's why Mark was visiting his childhood home. Because they were about to put it on the market, and he had some sweeping to do before they officially turned it into an *open house*. He was here to grab whatever item got left behind and forgotten.

He took a couple of boxes and bags and somehow gathered the strength to go inside. Just as he had feared, the moment he opened the door, reality hit him hard. He will never enter this house and be greeted with a smile. Another family would move in. They would create their own memories and the old ones – the ones that belonged to Mark and his family – would just disappear. The house will breathe them out through its walls and cracks, allowing them to vanish into thin air – never to be mentioned again.

The first thing he did – not because it was the most important thing, but because he feared that he would completely forget – was enter his parents' bedroom and scan for items left behind. He found an old shirt – probably his mother's, a pair of scissors, a house slippers, and a towel. *Much ado about nothing,* he thought as he was putting the stuff into a box. His mother, as much as he loved her, was a little bit controlling. Not in a bad way, but she always felt the need to check things twice, or make sure that everyone was playing their role the way they were supposed to. She had all the best intentions, of course, but some days, it seemed as though all she could do was order them around.

And just as he was about to leave the room, something from under the bed had caught his eye. It wasn't the mattress or a spring or anything like that. It seemed out of place – like it wasn't supposed to be where it was. Not a part of the bed, not a cover. He put the boxes he was carrying down and gently got closer to the bed. He kneeled to look under the bed. He was right. There was something hidden there. Could this be why his mother sent him to this room? But how could she know that he would even see this? What if he had just walked out of the door? Was it possible that this wasn't hers? That all this time, she had no idea that this was hiding under the bed she was sleeping on?

It was a notebook. The first thing he thought about was that it was his mother's journal. He had never seen her writing things down, but who knew? Women were capable of holding all sorts of secrets, weren't they? But then, as he inspected it closely, he realized that a journal is not what this notebook was. Nor was it his mother's. He remembered – all of a sudden, he remembered it all. It was his father's.

When Mark was a kid, his father would always carry around a silver notebook with him. Always writing things down, keeping notes. And the strangest thing of all was that this notebook was always with him. No matter where they would go, no matter what the time was. A L W A Y S – always. He remembered that even when they would having dinner, his father would just put down his knife and fork, grab his notebook and write a sentence or two down. And whenever Mark had asked him what that was, his father would just tell him that it was a work thing. But even at 11 years of age, Mark knew it couldn't be true. What could be a mechanic writing about during dinner?

The silver notebook had always remained a mystery. His father used to carry it around for a few years. Although he wasn't sure that it was just the one. Surely, he would run out of blank space after some time?

As he was holding that mysterious silver notebook now, so close to discovering what it was all about, what his father was writing down every day all those years ago, Mark didn't know if he could. Or should. What if he found some secrets that no kid should learn about their parents? What if it *was* a journal. A place where his father kept his darkest desires. Perhaps he would learn that he wasn't his real father, after all. All sorts of disturbing thoughts have taken over his mind, dancing around in circles, causing whirlwind-like fast emotions that couldn't be tamed. As he was getting panicky and anxiety started to kick in, he just bit the bullet and opened it.

The first thing he read was, "To my boy, Mark, and my beautiful wife, Ellena, thank you for your love and patience while it took forever for me to put my words to paper. I apologize for disrupted dinners, canceled parties, and long nights. This is for you! Love, Joseph!" As it turned out, it wasn't a journal. It was a book. Without even thinking about it, he sat on the floor and started reading.

It took him a couple of hours to finish reading the notebook. And yet, the story wasn't over. This was only the beginning, the first half of it, maybe. But where was the other half? He turned the room upside down. Searched drawers, inspected every inch of the bed, but all in vain. He didn't find the other notebook. If there ever was another half. What if his father just never finished it? But then he remembered all those years of writing things down, surely, he had written more than *that*.

He was beginning to get frustrated, and not only because he wasn't able to find his father's legacy. The thing that was, obviously, so important to him all of these years. But only because he was eager to find out how the story ends. The book was a heartfelt romance. The moment he realized it was a book, he immediately thought that something with a criminal background was written. But as the reading progressed, he was shocked to find out that it was actually romantic and really deep.

He never knew this side of his father. He always thought of him as the rough mechanic who loved western movies and old thrillers. Give him a Tom Cruise action, and he'd be happy. But this? This was definitely not something that he would expect. Not in a million years would he think that his father was able to put his heart and soul into this and write in such an elegant and beautiful manner.

The story was about two young lovers, separated by war, unable to find their way back to each other. Every feeling, every emotion was painted in such a real way that you couldn't help but feel it yourself. Every painful scene and every loss would hit you hard, smash your heart into pieces. Mark had surely crushed his – all he needed know was to know how the story ends so he could make it whole again.

But it was nowhere to be found. He had searched the whole whose – even the basement and the attic. But nothing. He couldn't find a single thing. There was only one thing left to try, and that was to call his mother and see if she knew this book existed.

When she finally picked up her phone – it always took some ringing before she could actually get to her phone – he explained everything. He told her how the first thing he checked was their bedroom, how he found some insignificant things like scissors there, but that there was also something he didn't hope to find. Not in a million years. And that was his father's book.

There was a moment of silence. She was probably quiet for about 10 seconds before she said, "I didn't know it was there. I never read it, you know. Because he always said that it wasn't finished. He was like that – always a perfectionist. Always keeping things in until he was sure they were constructed the right way. The things he said never came out wrong. He wasn't like me. Me? I keep nothing inside. If I am angry at something, I will be sure to let the whole world know. He loved that about me—my passion. I was the fire that got him going—his words, not mine. But, no. I honestly didn't know the book was there. How was it? Wait, don't tell me. I want to read it myself."

After that, Mark explained that he hadn't finished it either, because he only found one notebook. He read only the first part of the book, and it was mind-blowing. He then continued to explain his surprise to find out that his father had a soft side – something he had never seen. Mark also said how he turned the whole house upside down but found nothing. That's why he was calling, to see if she maybe knew where the other notebook would be hidden.

"Honestly, I have no idea. He left this world peacefully in his sleep. We never got the chance to say goodbye, and that's what hurts me most. I haven't been able to sleep in our bed since he passed away, which is why I have never found the notebook. As for the other two, I don't know." She said.

"Two? So, there are three notebooks?" Mark asked, surprised.

"Yes. He finished three of the silver notebooks. The last part was finished a couple of years back. I had asked him about it a few times, but he would always find a way to change the subject. I thought that the book didn't end up the way he thought it would, so I never asked again. But wait! He was working on that last part while we were at the lake house. Perhaps he left them there," his mother explained.

Mark knew what he had to do. He went inside the house to clean up the mess he had made earlier while looking for the notebook. He also finished what he had come there in the first place. To get all of the things they have left behind so that the house would be ready for showing. Once all of that was taken care of, he had one more thing he needed to do – to check the lake house.

Their lake house was about an hour away from his childhood home. But even if it took him days to get there, he knew that there would be nothing that could change his mind at this moment. It was something he needed to do. Not only so he could honor his father's memory, but also because he needed to keep this new side of his father alive. The book would be proof of the softness he never knew, and so he would always keep it close to heart and nurture it dearly.

It was almost nightfall when he finally got to the lake house. The streets here were empty at this time of the day and at this time of the year. In summer, there would be tourists crowding the place, young couples exchanging kisses on the bench nearby, families with children enjoying the beautiful weather. But all was quiet here in early December.

This was the second empty and cold house that he stepped into today, but this was usual for their lake house. They had never lived there. His parents had bought this while he was still young, so they would have a quick getaway. Someplace they could come and visit quickly, without major preparations. The perfect weekend escape.

When she entered the door, the first thing that noticed was the staleness of it. The air that had been trapped inside, the walls that were screaming for a breath of fresh oxygen. He opened the windows wide, despite the chilly weather outside. He hardly even noticed it, for he had more important things on his mind now.

The house, compared to his childhood home, was relativelty small. Two smaller bedrooms, a living room, a kitchen, and a bathroom. No attic place, just as small basement. He started in the living room. He looked under the couch, inspected the shelves, went through the junk drawer – nothing. Then, he moved to their bedroom. The obvious place to look was under the bed, as that was how he had found the first notebook. However, this time, he had no luck – they weren't here. But as soon as he saw the table nook in the corner of the room, he knew that he had hit the jackpot.

Sure enough, the notebooks were there. Not hidden behind, not taped underneath it. Just placed inside the drawer. He opened the one that was on the top, and he saw the number "3" written on the first page. That meant that this was the notebook number three, so he put it aside for later. He needed to read the second book first.

He started reading the first couple of pages when he realized that it was actually getting dark outside. His wife will worry if he wasn't home in a reasonable time, so he took the notebooks with him, with the hope of reading them back home.

And that's what he did. After they had finished their dinner and put their kids to sleep, Mark shared the story with his wife. She couldn't believe it either, as she also remembered how Joseph was always rough around the edges. His romantic side surely came as a shock.

He was also eager to read the book, so Mark gave her the first notebook, and he started reading the second one. His wife was long asleep when he finally finished the whole thing. The ending was everything he had hoped for and more.

It wasn't because it was his father who had actually written it. Nor because he wanted to somehow keep his father's spirit alive. No, the writing was genuinely beautiful. The story was crafted in such a thoughtful way, that he had to remind himself that this was actually his father's book, not something he had picked up at the library. For Mark, this was one of the best books he had ever read.

So the next thing he needed to do was pretty obvious. He had to contact a few publishing houses and see if he could find an agent that will be compelled with the story as he was. He wanted his father's work to be recognized and respected, even if he was no longer around to get the credit for his book.

He contacted a professional to help him send out a manuscript at a couple of agencies. Now, all Mark had to do was wait. Wait for a response, wait to see if other people liked his father's book as much as he enjoyed reading it.

Three weeks had passed when an agency finally responded to his request. It was a well-known publishing house, so he was feeling very nervous when he was opening his mail. When the word "Congratulations" caught his attention, he couldn't believe his happiness.

Six months later, her father's book was officially available. Now the world would know something that he waited until after his father's death to find out. That not everything was as it seemed. Sometimes, those who act tough are the softest inside. We cannot peek into anyone's soul – all we can do is support and love the ones closest to us so they can reveal what's on their inside, on their own.

All Aboard the Night Train

Duration: 30 minutes

There was something about traveling at night that soothed Eleanor. She didn't know exactly why that was. Maybe it was because of the street lights – passing through and seeing these dots of light change as she moved at a fast speed was quite calming. Or perhaps it was all those people that were dozed off in the train – observing other passengers defeated after a long day and soundly asleep used to make her sleepy, too. Or simply it was because of the mere fact that it was nighttime – one should sleep at night, wasn't that right? Whatever the reason, traveling at night always seemed to make her drift away minutes after the ride started. But tonight, sleep didn't come as quickly.

It was 10 PM when she boarded the train. She was supposed to arrive at her destination in the wee hours, so she had plenty of time to get some rest. But somehow, even despite the fact that she had had a busy and long day, she couldn't stop her racing mind. So she did every trick she had in her bag. From breathing deeply to counting sheep, she literally tried everything she could think of. And yet, nothing helped.

Her eyes were wide open, and her mind as sharp as in the morning. Did he drink too much coffee? Was there too much sugar in that small piece of candy she took a couple of hours ago? Why on earth couldn't she fall asleep?

If this was a normal day, and she was on vacation, traveling to a far place, ready to spend days doing absolutely nothing, not sleeping tonight would not be an issue. Not at all. But, unfortunately, that was not the case. A lot was at stake here. Perhaps her entire future depended on this night. So having a good shuteye and getting rest so that she could be recharged in the morning was of vital importance at this point. Because this was not a pleasure trip – it was actually of professional nature.

Eleanor was an aspiring actress. She had a couple of significant roles, but nothing that major that would get her recognized. She was 23 years old, and wanted to build a serious acting career. That was what she was trying to change tomorrow. Tomorrow was the audition of her lifetime. If she could kand this role, she could quit her job at Stacey's and make a living out of what she loved to do. Stacey's was a local diner that was owned by her mother's friend. Eleanor had been working there since high-school, but she was dying for that to change. She never saw her in the serving industry – she wanted to be on the big screen. Making people laugh, cry. Delivering emotions while playing roles that her audience could relate too.

The audition that she was getting ready for was for the leading role in a thriller TV show. She couldn't stop but thinking about what it would feel like if she got the part. All of the fans that she would have gained, the recognition she would have attained. She wasn't a shallow person – didn't care for the fame and money. Since she was a little girl, everyone had been saying to her how she had great acting skills. In school plays, she would always get the main part. Her teachers would always compliment her acting, reading, reciting, and so it was only natural that she would move into that direction. Because since she was a little girl, acting was something that made her truly happy.

As time passed, she was starting to get more and more nervous. She started obsessing over every detail of the audition – about her posture, the way she would talk, whether to have her head down, things of that nature. But that was not the only thing. The main reason why Eleanor was feeling down now was that she knew that if she didn't sleep at all tonight, it would result in a lack of energy and underperforming. So, it was only understandable how stressful this ride was to her.

But, the more and more she was thinking about the audition, the role, and the fact that she wasn't feeling sleepy at all, only made her more anxious. So she decided that she needed to distract herself in order to trick her mind into taking a break and finding a way to relax.

She took out the phone, but that was only more stressful than distracting, so she decided against it. She put it back in her pocket. Just as she was starting to feel her anxiety piling up inside, loud noises caught her attention.

Two men, one younger, no more than 30 years old, and one in his late 50s perhaps, had started an argument over a seat. The old man was sitting in the young man's seat and wouldn't change it, even after the young man had asked politely and explained that he would rather sit in the seat written on the ticket. What started out as a polite request quickly turned into a heated disagreement. It wasn't until the conductor came that peace was finally restored.

Eleanor realized that, for a minute there, she got distracted. As it turned out, observing other people made her forget about her worries for a second. So she thought, *why not try this for a little while longer?*

And that's exactly what she did. She thought it'd be best to start with the person sitting next to her. It was a younger girl, perhaps 19 or 20 years old. She kept checking her phone and had a worried look on her face, so Eleanor assumed that he had maybe gotten into a fight with someone. Perhaps, her boyfriend. But where was she going? Maybe she was returning home? Or was it the other way around. Maybe she had left her home to sneak out and be with her boyfriend. Then her phone rang, and Eleanor just couldn't help but overhear the conversation. It wasn't that she was eavesdropping – the girl was sitting right next to her, so it was impossible not to overhear.

As it turned out, she didn't guess. It wasn't a love quarrel or a family issue. She was actually fired from work over something that had nothing to do with her. She had lost her apartment and was going back home to her parents, where she hoped she would find a job and save some money from not paying rent for a while.

The next person that Eleanor decided to observe was sitting in front of her. It was a younger man, in his late 20s or early 30s, she couldn't tell. He was good-looking and looked healthy. Which is perhaps a result of following a strict diet. She noticed how carefully he was reading the food label of the healthy snack he had bought.

Next to him was an older lady. She kept looking at pictures of young children, and Eleanor immediately assumed they were her grandkids. Perhaps she hadn't seen them in a while and was now traveling to spend time with them. She noticed how her facial expression would change with each photo, turning into a half-smile, softening up her wrinkles, making her eyes sparkle. Eleanor's heart melted a bit, and she immediately remembered her 90-year old grandmother. She missed her very much.

Then, she moved onto a man in his early 60s, maybe. He was reading an actual newspaper, which was rare these days with all these devices and electronic readers. The other thing she noticed was that he was sharp-dressed and was wearing a hat. Which was also something that you don't get to see these days. The man looked like he got somehow transported from 1955, and that seemed especially charming to her. She loved the golden age of Hollywood. Her all-time celebrity crush was Carry Grant, so this man immediately reminded her of his movies. The seat next to the man was empty, which is where she had placed his antique brown bag, which made the whole picture even more charming.

All of a sudden, she opened her eyes to see that the man wasn't there. Her brown bag was all gone. She looked at her watch only to discover that 4 hours had passed. She actually dozed off. She was to arrive in an hour, so she was glad that she was able to get some rest. When the train would reach her stop, she would get some breakfast, a cup of coffee, and go through the script she had prepared for the audition.

She realized that everything was better if you were not stressing over it. Sometimes, no matter how worried you were about something, the best you could do was just distract yourself and let your mind reset on its own.

Chain of Rocks

Duration: 30 minutes

Jim was 60 when he started the adventure of watching bald eagles. It wasn't because it was something that he had always wanted to do – it wasn't a big hobby or desire of his. It actually was the opposite. He always thought that waiting with your binoculars to spot this bird come and eat was not only a waste of time but also pretty silly. Why would a grown man want to be spending his time like this? Why on earth was my dad doing this for so many years?

You see, he started this adventure to honor his dad's spirit, in a way. Watching eagles – or any other bird, for that matter – was a huge passion of his father's. When Jim was a kid, he used to watch his dad talk about this with such excitement, that one would think it was the most interesting thing in the world. He had only taken Jim with him on this adventure once, but the weather had worked against them, and their trip had to be cut short. Shortly after that, Jim's dad had passed away.

So Jim had no one to teach him the proper way to do this – he learned all there was to know on the internet, although, as he was not a big fan of technology, he wasn't quite sure he understood it all. He never thought he would here, ever, but as retirement got closer, his perspective in life shifted. So there he was, with the binoculars in his hands, getting ready for a trip that his father would think to be the most exciting in the world.

At first, Jim thought that he would have to travel to the other side of the continent to find a great observing spot, but the truth was, one of the best places was just a stone throw away. Here in St. Louis, in the city where Jim had spent all of his life.

The best place where one could observe bald eagles come to fish in open water was situated on the north edge of St. Louis. And it was actually a bridge.

The *Chain of Rocks* bridge covers the Mississippi River, offering a crossing point for bikers and walkers. Although it was mainly a part of the old US Route 66, no traffic was allowed over the bridge anymore. It got transferred to the New Chain of Rocks Bridge, which was constructed in 1966 solely for this purpose. The historic bridge, however, remained reserved only for the walkers passing through.

At one end, the bridge was situated in the Missouri shoreline, while on the eastern end, Chain of Rocks was a part of the Chouteau Island, which was in

Madison, Illinois. The length o the bridge was a little bit over 5,300 feet, so it was not so bad for a man in his 60s to cross.

The name, *Chain of Rocks*, came from the large shoal beneath the bridge, which made this part of the river hard to navigate. Although this chain of rocks was barely visible today, thanks to the low-water dam, if you were lucky enough to be passing through during extremely low water conditions, you would be able to see it.

The best thing about the old Chain of Rocks bridge was its 22-degree bend that occurred right in the middle of the crossing and offered an excellent vantage point. Jim had crossed this bridge a couple of times before in his life, but he never knew that people – as passionate as his father was – actually came here to observe bald eagles in the Mississipi waters.

He was also surprised to know that this was a *free* program as well. You didn't only have the opportunity to come here whenever you wanted between late December and early March, but you also had the opportunity to be a part of a live Educational Program at a certain date in January.

During this program, not only would the local volunteers explain in detail everything one would need to know about the bald eagles, but they would also put on a great show that people seemed to find quite amusing. So Jim had to give it a try. It wasn't as raw of experience as his father would sign up for, but since he knew nothing about eagle watching, nor he was a big fan of nature, to be honest, he thought that the Chain of Rocks was the best starting point.

The program urged the visitors to bring their binoculars, cameras, and not forget to dress for the cold weather. The wind tended to get harsh during winter there, so it was wise to bring warm clothes and not let the low temperature interrupt the one-of-a-kind experience.

But that was not all the locals had prepared for the visitors. At the entrance of the bridge – at the Missouri side of it – every year, there would be Lewis and Clark re-enactors from the Corps of Discovery. These local entertainers would demonstrate the history and show how Lewis and Clark used to live, and how their crew traveled two hundred years ago.

The thing Jim appreciated the most was the fact that there were also viewing scopes set up. Trained locals would be there to help the visitors find the best spots for observing and also assist them in getting the most from their viewing, in terms of close-up shots or any other requests they had.

On the Illinois side of the bridge, the Lewis and Clark re-enactors came from the Lewis and Clark State Historic Site in Hartford.

The Chain of Rocks was one of the many great spots for Eagle Watching in this part of the country. Every year, between December and March, thousands of bald eagles would come to migrate to the Illinois and Mississipi Rivers. There would be plenty of spots (and times) to observe them, but Jim liked this opportunity the best. Not only because it was relatively close to his home, but also because he felt like he was in need of professional help. He wanted so desperately to finally find out what his father thought to be so exciting.

He had tried this a couple of times, though. Although not with eagles in particular, but birds in general. A couple of times, while he was camping with his family in the woods, we would sneak out early in the morning with his binoculars, find a quiet place to sit and just observe. He hadn't seen anything super special. Just regular birds that he would also spot in the city, while sitting on a bench in the park.

But this felt different. Deeper, somehow. For the first time, in his 60-year life, he was close to discovering what his father would talk so passionately about. Perhaps that is why he had never gathered the strength to go eagle watching before. Because he knew himself. He knew that he was no fan of adventures in nature. He knew that, if he found this to be not worth it, he would somehow lose the little connection and vague memory of his father that he was so desperately trying to still keep alive. He may be 60 years old, but the love he felt for his late father was as deep as it was when he was no older than 6.

But as he was getting closer to retiring, he also realized that he couldn't be really, truly connected to his father if he, for all of his life, hadn't given the thing that was so important to his father, a shot. And so he decided. He would spend most of the 19th of January with his binoculars in his hand, watching eagles from the Chain of Rocks bridge.

Although the Lewis and Clark show was surely entertaining, he couldn't wait to discover the beauty of the eagles. Once he was shown the perfect spot for observing and he put the binoculars on – he finally was able to see what it was all about. It was absolutely exhilarating. Seeing these birds, as rare as they were, to migrate and fish in these cold waters was absolutely an experience he would never forget. He only wished that his father was here to tell him that he finally understood. That he was now able to see what he would always talk about. The beauty of it. The innocence. The joy to be witnessing something so pure. It was a true blessing.

He would now go home and call his daughter, for he had found a new passion to talk about. A new thing to share with her. Something that, he hoped, she would gladly remember him by, Something that, sometime in the future, she might even decide to try on her own. As a way to honor her father and keep Jim's memory alive. It was a good thought. A good day. And he was glad he finally got around to doing it. *Better late than never*, was what he was thinking about as he got off the Chain of Rocks Bridge and headed home.

Conclusion

Thank you for giving this book a shot! I hope that the meditations have helped you train your mind and body to better relax and relieve the stress so that you can rest in a healthy way. I also hope that you barely got to the end of the stories and that they have been successful in giving you the shut-eye you need.

If you found this book to be helpful, would you please leave a review and let others know? Your feedback is what keeps me writing and dreaming, and it is always greatly appreciated!

Sweet dreams!

www.ingramcontent.com/pod-product-compliance
Lightning Source LLC
Chambersburg PA
CBHW070909080526
44589CB00013B/1241